Breaking Open the Gospel of Luke

Gerard P. Weber and Robert L. Miller

Breaking Open the Gospel of Luke

ST.
ANTHONY
MESSENGER
PRESS

CINCINNATI, OHIO

Nihil Obstat: Rev. Edward Gratsch
　　　　　　　Rev. Hilarion Kistner, O.F.M.

Imprimi Potest: John Bok, O.F.M.
　　　　　　　Provincial

Imprimatur: +James H. Garland, V.G.
　　　　　　　Archdiocese of Cincinnati
　　　　　　　August 13, 1990

The *nihil obstat* and *imprimatur* are a declaration that a book is considered to be free from doctrinal or moral error. It is not implied that those who have granted the *nihil obstat* and *imprimatur* agree with the contents, opinions or statements expressed.

Scripture selections are taken from *The New American Bible With Revised New Testament*, copyright ©1986 by the Confraternity of Christian Doctrine, Washington, D.C., and are used with permission. All rights reserved.

The passage from *Once More Astonished: The Parables of Jesus Christ* by Jan Lambrecht, copyright ©1981 by Jan Lambrecht, is reprinted by permission of The Crossroad Publishing Company.

The passage written by Louis Cameli taken from the April 1988 issue of *Chicago Studies* is reprinted by permission of *Chicago Studies.*

Cover and book design by Julie Lonneman

Illustration by Stephen D. Kroeger and Julie Lonneman

ISBN 0-86716-138-8

©1990, Gerard P. Weber, S.T.L., and Robert Miller, S.T.L.

Published by St. Anthony Messenger Press

Contents

Introduction

AFTER CREATING THE SEED-BEARING PLANTS and the trees, according to one story, God went for a walk in the Garden. God came to the oak tree and found its branches drooping in despair. Asked what was wrong, the oak replied that it was depressed because it was not tall and straight like the fir tree. God walked over to the fir tree. It was shaking with anger because it could not stand being so ugly and having prickly needles instead of beautiful leaves like the cherry tree. But the cherry tree told God it was disgusted with itself because, no matter how hard it tried, its fruit was always small with a hard pit in the middle. It did not have big, juicy fruit like the apple tree. God strode over to the apple tree and found it complaining that its fruit was the wrong color—not bright like the orange.

Saddened, God sat on a rock to rest. God had tried so hard to plant a beautiful, diverse garden and no one was satisfied. All that could be heard were complaints. Sitting there and brooding, God caught sight of a daisy growing between two stones. It was happy, smiling, waving with the wind. God asked if the daisy had any complaints. "None," said the cheerful little flower. "I figured you made me to be a daisy and all I want to be is the best daisy I can be." God walked on, cheered at the success of creation, and decided to take a chance on making man and woman.

In some way everyone asks the question, "What will give me a complete and fulfilling life? What will make me be the 'best me'?" Where do we go to find out how to be the "best me"? Many different answers are offered by the media, the culture, the people around us. Many of these are enticing. They promise quick fulfillment and instant happiness, but in time they fail to produce and are seen to be too simplistic and superficial.

The satisfaction level in our life depends on our vision of ourselves and of the world in which we live, on our philosophy of life. Our vision of life emerges as we interact with the images of life projected by the various communities of which we are a part. The degree to which we buy into the images projected by these communities molds and shapes our personal vision, our idea of the "best me."

Over the past several thousand years many people have turned to the Scriptures for help in finding a vision which makes sense out of life and brings happiness and fulfillment. Many have found there a vision which puts some order into the chaos and confusion of seemingly random events in life, a philosophy which helps them see clearly the ambiguities of daily life and accept the contradictions they encounter in themselves and in others.

This book picks up that quest. It looks at just one scriptural book—the Gospel of Luke—to explore the vision of life projected by Jesus. And it focuses on just one aspect of Luke's message: the stories he tells. We will look at the images and sayings in these stories in search of a view of life and the world which will help us to find meaning and personal satisfaction in life.

Along the way you will be asked to pause and take stock. The reflection questions serve best as starting points for sharing and discussing with others the ideas in each section, although you may consider them alone.

1) *Find a picture in a magazine of what you think you would be like if you were the best possible you.*

2) *What have you done in the past 24 hours to show this side of yourself?*

3) *Name three or four attitudes about life projected by the media and our culture that work for or against your best you. Do you think these attitudes are reflected in Scripture?*

The Bishops' Invitation

Many Catholics, hungry for a better vision of life, realize that Jesus offers that vision. They want to know more about him and to grow closer to him in order to have a more complete and satisfying life. One place they seek him is in Scripture.

At the same time, some Catholics feel uncomfortable picking up the Bible on their own. They fear reading meaning into the text because they have always depended on the Church to explain the texts. But recent popes have urged Catholics to study the Bible. The bishops at the Second Vatican Council wrote, "This sacred synod earnestly...urges all the Christian faithful...to learn by frequent reading of the divine Scriptures the 'excelling knowledge of Jesus Christ' (Phil 3:6). 'For ignorance of Scripture is ignorance of Christ' " (*Constitution on Divine Revelation*, #25).

A Catholic must know the Scriptures to realize that the Church is a biblical Church. Even those things which are distinctly Catholic—such as devotion to Mary, the Mass, Reconciliation and modern Church teachings on social justice—have a solid biblical basis.

Other Catholics feel uncomfortable opening the Scriptures because they think they need to be scholars to read it with profit. They are afraid that they do not have the necessary background. But scholarship is not necessary. The bishops do warn readers to have regard for the literary forms "[f]or truth is expressed in a variety of ways, depending on whether a text is history of one kind or another, or whether its form is that of prophecy, poetry or some other type of speech" (*Constitution on Revelation*, #12).

In most cases common sense helps the reader realize that truth is expressed differently in poetry or prophecy than in a letter or in a story. But the bishops' advice puts Catholics on guard against reading the Scriptures in a very literal way, believing that the words always mean exactly what they appear to say. The literal approach does not allow for the way the meaning of words changes in translation, how they are conditioned by historical conditions and how people of different cultures think and write.

An approach which takes each word literally and sees each word or each verse standing on its own apart from the rest of Scripture can be very confusing. One verse may seemingly contradict or obscure the meaning of another. For example, "Beat your plowshares into swords,/and your pruning hooks into spears;/let the weak man say, 'I am a warrior!' " (Joel 4:10); "They shall beat their swords into plowshares/and their spears into pruning hooks;/One nation shall not raise the sword against another,/nor shall they train for war again" (Isaiah 2:4).

Which of these images, people of peace or people of war, is really the image God is presenting? To understand such contradictory verses fully, it is necessary to understand the times in which they were written. This, of course, is the type of help the scholar offers, and it is not difficult to come by. Many easy-to-read, nontechnical commentaries briefly give such information.[1]

The bishops gave two more simple bits of advice. They said that to understand any passage in Scripture "serious

---

[1]See the Bibliography on page 101.

4

attention must be given to the content and unity of the whole of Scripture, if the meaning of the sacred text is to be correctly brought to light." In other words, no text stands by itself, but must be seen in the wider context of the entire Bible. The bishops went on to say that "the living tradition of the whole Church must be taken into account" (*Constitution on Revelation*, #12). Those who rely solely on the words of Scripture as they read them forget that the Holy Spirit has been working in the Church for 2,000 years to help people understand God's word more and more fully. Catholics have been exposed to this living tradition through religious education, sermons, homilies, retreats and so on. When they pick up the Bible, this tradition helps guide them in understanding the word of God.

FOR REFLECTION

1) Rate the following statements on a scale of 1 to 10, 1 being totally different from your idea of what Scripture is and 10 being closest to your idea.

___*The Holy Spirit has guided the whole of Scripture but has allowed individuals the freedom to write in their own style and from their own cultural and historical viewpoint.*

___*The Scriptures are a factual and accurate report of what happened and of what people said.*

___*The Scriptures are an accurate report of scientific facts and of what will occur in the future.*

___*It is difficult for the ordinary person to understand the message of Scripture.*

___*Scripture contains all the truths one needs for salvation.*

___*Scripture, prayer, community and Eucharist are the necessary foundations of spiritual growth.*

After reading and discussing this book, come back to
these questions and see whether you would rate the
statements in the same way.

2) *What apprehensions do you have about opening the*
   Scriptures?

3) *What do you expect to gain from exploring the Gospel*
   of Luke?

A Five-Step Approach to Scripture

Two basic approaches to Scripture can lead a person to
a deeper union with the Lord. The first begins with the
words and incidents in Scripture. A person reads a passage
and asks, "What does this mean in my life? How do I apply
it to my situation?" We call this approach "bringing
Scripture to life."

The other, "bringing life to Scripture," begins with a
life situation, problem or question. The reader searches the
words and incidents in Scripture for words which address
his or her circumstances or concerns.

A great many people try the first approach, bringing
Scripture to bear on life. Sometimes it works. The text seems
to speak directly to a situation or problem they are facing,
and they experience illumination and affirmation.

But at other times the words they read leave them
feeling cold and empty. The passage does not connect with
their present or past experience. They find no
enlightenment, no comfort. This problem of making a text
relevant to life is most often experienced at liturgy. If the
homilist's words do not resonate with people's situation or
experience, they feel bored or cheated.

The second approach, bringing life to Scripture, is
much more dynamic. It is also more demanding; it requires
getting in touch with one's life, culture and environment by
a certain amount of reflection before picking up the Bible.

It begins with a question or problem. Not necessarily something personal which is directly and urgently screaming for attention—death, illness, loss of work—it may be a problem which the TV and newspapers are reporting: crime, nuclear arms, war, homelessness, unjust distribution of resources, abortion, AIDS, drugs, broken families. Our response to all situations, personal or social, will either be illumined and guided by the images and the sayings of Scripture understood in the context of the Church's tradition or it will be guided by personal preference and the prevailing culture.

Our first reaction to a great many problems—personal or global—is often to feel helplessness and despair. We say, "There is nothing I can do! How can one person do anything about such a huge problem?" The response prompted by the "life to Scripture" approach is to ask further questions: "What kind of person does Scripture call me to be in this situation? In what direction is the Scripture pointing me? What image presented by Scripture will help me in this situation?"

This approach requires time—time to think about one's life, time to look up and reflect on the Scripture stories. It works best when one develops the discipline of doing it on a regular basis.

Here's an example of how it works. You pick up the Sunday newspaper and read about the hungry in the world. There are stories about people starving in Ethiopia, of malnutrition in poor children living in the U.S., of people dying from hunger on the streets of Calcutta. At this point you can lay down the newspaper with a sigh of gratitude that you have sufficient food, a decent job and home, a prosperous country. Or you can bring life to Scripture.

Step One: Ask. Put the situation into a question: "What can I do? I am but one well-fed person living in a fairly prosperous community. What can a person like me do in the face of world hunger?"

Step Two: Find the scriptural parallel. Look for a story in the Scriptures alluding to a similar situation, the need to feed many people with no apparent resources. Ask if Jesus confronted a similar situation in his life.

The story of the multiplication of the loaves comes to mind. In that incident, people had followed Jesus all day and were hungry. They were in a deserted place and some distance from a place where they could buy food. The disciples recognized the problem but could see no way of feeding the crowd. The only solution they saw was to send the people away hungry. Jesus would not hear of this. He challenged the disciples to "give them something to eat yourselves." This did not seem much of an answer to the apostles; all they could find were five loaves and two fish. Jesus told the people to sit down and relax. He blessed what the disciples had and they distributed the loaves and fish until all had eaten. It was amazing: The little they had had become enough to satisfy a hungry crowd (see Luke 9:10-17).

Step Three: Seek fuller understanding. Check other passages which bear on this situation. Footnotes and cross-references in any recent edition of the Bible reveal that this story occurs in five other places in the New Testament. Read the other passages and watch more details emerge. For example, Mark 6:34-44 says that Jesus looked on the crowd with pity because they were "like sheep without a shepherd"—an image which recalls Jesus calling himself the Good Shepherd in John 10.

At this point, you can read a commentary to throw more light on the question by explaining the various passages in light of what scholars think Jesus actually said and what points the various evangelists were trying to make. Or you might decide to follow the footnotes for John 10 to Psalm 23, which speaks of the Lord as a shepherd who leads his sheep to green pastures and "sets a table before them." By this time the image of compassion in the face of hunger certainly is emerging.

The question of how to make do with very little still remains. The more familiar you are with Scripture, the more passages will come to mind. For example, Isaiah 58:6-8 speaks of sharing one's bread with the hungry, sheltering the oppressed and homeless as a way of letting one's light break forth like dawn. 1 Kings 17:7-16 tells the story of a poor widow who shared what little she had with the prophet Elijah. The Lord rewarded her by promising through the prophet that she would not run out of flour or oil till the famine in the land of Israel was over. The image of a God faithful to the generous emerges.

Step Four: Reflect. You realize that hunger is not a new issue, but was all too well known to the people of the Bible. Several strong images emerge: concern, trust in the Lord, doing what little one can.

Step Five: Take action. Finally, you are ready to answer the question of what to do. It may be to bring food to a food distribution center on a regular basis, to offer time at a soup kitchen, to organize a food drive or to contribute to an organization which feeds the hungry. One person collected unsold sandwiches from several catering companies and trucked them across the border to Mexican children. He answered the call of Scripture, using what little he had—a persuasive tongue and an old truck—to feed many hungry mouths.

This, of course, is not the only way to approach Scripture, but it does assure that you begin with something that is relevant to your own life, that you do not attempt to solve problems by quoting a single text out of context and that you have at least a modicum of help from scholarly research. It brings together various images from the Scriptures which in time will mold your character not in the image of pop stars and TV advertisers but in the image of Jesus.

FOR REFLECTION

Try this five-step approach with a question or problem you have:

1) Write down the question or problem in a few words.

2) Think of a Scripture story in which someone has faced a similar question or problem.

3) Search for related stories or passages that may shed additional light on your situation. Use the footnotes and cross-references in your Bible to help find them.

4) Reflect and pray over these passages, asking yourself, "In what way do these passages help me clarify my situation?"

5) Decide what you might do as a result of searching the Scriptures.

" May God add His blessing to the reading of these words : "

Chapter One
The Call

THE "BRINGING LIFE TO SCRIPTURE" APPROACH has been at times used by people in a frivolous way. They open the Bible at random and blindly pick a text to find an answer to a question or problem. An extreme example of this approach would be a gambler who blindly picks a text as a clue to the winner of the Kentucky Derby. Even if such a one can establish a link between the text and the name of a horse, it is hard to believe that God is actually helping pick a winner.

This approach has also been used by people who have more serious problems but who are looking for a clear-cut answer to their question or a definite solution to their problem. For example, a person who is married to an alcoholic or has a child on drugs asks, "What am I to do?" Seldom can a direct answer to day-by-day questions such as these be found in a Scripture text.

The real answer usually comes from reflection on several passages in Scripture and emerges in the form of an attitude to be cultivated. Thus, thinking about the stories in the Book of Judges of how God treated the Israelites when they fell away from the covenant time and time again along with Jesus' story of the Prodigal Son (or the prodigal— recklessly extravagant—father) might well lead a person to an attitude of "tough love," of allowing the other to "hit bottom" while waiting for the appropriate time to intervene.

Our five-step approach is most helpful, however, for

help in answering the most basic questions about life—questions about the origin and nature of human beings, about the existence and nature of God, about the nature and role of Jesus, etc. In some way or other everyone asks, "Who am I?" and "How do I live the most complete and fulfilling life?" Often people are satisfied with superficial, simplistic or ready-made cultural answers. But for those who are not so easily satisfied, the Scriptures do sketch a startling answer.

In telling the story of Jesus all four evangelists were really proposing an answer to these two questions. It is clear from their words that they were writing to people who identified themselves as Christians. Thus the person of Jesus was to be the core, the center, of their lives. Following the way of Jesus was to be the road to a complete and fulfilling life. The evangelists wrote for people of the first century. They wrote for people of differing backgrounds: Jew and Gentile, slave and free, rich and poor, city folk and farmers. But the answers they gave still hold true for us when we ask the same questions about our identity and the meaning of our lives. In the evangelists' answers we find no neat definitions of who we are or specific instructions about what we are to do. Instead we have stories and sayings of Jesus which evoke images and which, through reflection, need to be applied to our individual lives.

No one can adequately answer the question "Who am I?" in one sentence or even in a thousand-page autobiography. Too many different characteristics, qualities, memories, experiences and even physical facts go into that one answer to capture the totality of a person. Even if all a person's characteristics were completely described, it would be impossible to give an honest appraisal of the value placed on each of these characteristics. Two people describe themselves as musicians: one may be a Beethoven, the other a third-rate drummer in a knocked-together rock group. Two people can describe themselves as being concerned about others: Mother Teresa of Calcutta and the local Mafia boss. Two people can call themselves Christians: one who denies the divinity of Christ, the other John Paul II.

Searching the Scriptures for the answer to the questions "Who am I?" and "What am I to do?" will give us an image, a standard, against which we can compare our own answers.

1) Draw a line with the date of your birth at one end and the present date at the other. Put an X on the line at the ages when you asked questions about who you are and where you are going.

2) What two questions do you have at the present about who you are and where you are going?

3) Write down without reflection or censoring all the possible words (good or bad, desirable or not) which describe what you want out of life.

4) Next, go through the list above and cross out half the words, the half which you think are less important. Repeat this process of crossing out half of the remaining words till you have only one or two words left. What have you done within the last week to achieve these values?

Who Is This Jesus?

Luke wrote his Gospel to a friend we only know as Theophilus, "Beloved of God." But we can be assured that Theophilus must have been asking questions which, in the last analysis, boiled down to queries about his identity and about how he was to live as a Christian. We might imagine Theophilus saying something like this to Luke: "I have heard your preaching, but if I am to be a Christian I have some questions to which I would like an answer. Who is this Jesus?

13

How do I know that what you say about him is true? What will it mean in my life if I say that I am a Christian?"

Luke did more for his friend than make a simple statement about the nature of Jesus or give the factual details of his 33 years of life. Luke wanted Theophilus really to know and understand Jesus. By knowing Jesus, by affirming Jesus as Lord and Messiah, by accepting salvation and the call to discipleship, Theophilus would come to know himself better. He would see himself in a new light. He would realize God's wondrous love for him and the tremendous dignity that was his. He would also see other people and the whole world in a different way. To help his friend, Luke used traditional stories, memories of older people and collections of writings which were current in his community. He assures his friend that he has checked their authenticity by consulting eyewitnesses.

The beginning of the story Luke tells (1:5—2:52) differs greatly from the only other infancy narrative, Matthew's. Many details are the same: the names of Jesus, Mary and Joseph, Bethlehem as the place of Jesus' birth, Nazareth as the town in which the child grew up. Many others are different: Joseph's doubt, the flight into Egypt, Herod's murderous rage, the visit of the Magi. Neither of the two evangelists were concerned with bare biographical facts. Luke and Matthew were both concerned with showing who Jesus is and what he means in the lives of those who choose to follow him. Their answer is the same: Jesus is the long awaited Messiah; Jesus is the son of God; fulfillment and peace are found in following him.

Writing, as a *New American Bible* footnote puts it, "in imitation of Old Testament birth stories, combining historical and legendary details, literary ornamentation and interpretation of Scripture," Luke answers up front the question, "Who is Jesus?" The angel who appears to Zechariah brushes aside the suggestion that anything is impossible to God. This sterile couple will have a son who will go before the one who is to come, the Messiah. This same angel declares that the son born of Mary will be called "Son of the Most High." Elizabeth greets Mary by asking, "And how does this happen to me, that the mother of my Lord should come to me?" (1:43). The shepherds hear the angel call the newborn babe "Messiah and Lord" (2:11). Old Simeon is assured by the Holy Spirit that the child he is holding is the Messiah, "a light for revelation to the Gentiles,/ and glory for your people Israel" (2:32). Finally, the young boy Jesus stays for three days in his "Father's house" (2:49).

Luke did not write a theological treatise about the nature of Jesus. He couldn't. Our theological understanding has taken centuries to develop and is still today being refined. Luke spoke to his friend in stories full of references to the hopes of the Jews which clarified for him the identity of Jesus. If Theophilus accepts Luke's assessment of Jesus, he will begin to see himself more clearly as a follower of the Way, as a Christian. So will we.

FOR REFLECTION

1) *Read Luke's Infancy Narrative (1:26—2:52). What do the various titles of Jesus say to you about who he is and what his role is?*

—*Lord*

—*Messiah*

—*Son of the Most High*

—*A light of revelation to the Gentiles*

—*The glory of Israel*

—*The one who must be in his Father's house*

2) *What do these titles say to you about who you are?*

Theme Statements

In the infancy narratives Luke also begins to lay out for Theophilus what is required of a disciple of Jesus. He introduces the major themes which he will come back to time and time again and develop more fully in the rest of his story. These themes are most helpful in answering the second question about how one must live to walk in the way of Jesus.

For example, the circumstances of Jesus' birth reflect Luke's theme of Jesus' sympathy for and identity with the poor, the social outcasts. He does not tell this story as a call for a social revolution but as a challenge to adopt an attitude which makes it impossible for the disciple to treat the poor and outcast as less than fully human.

Another theme helpful for the disciple is that of journey. Luke shows Jesus' journey beginning in Mary's womb. Jesus will travel to Jerusalem to die. In Luke's second volume, the Acts of the Apostles, Jesus will continue his journey to the center of the Roman Empire, Rome, and throughout the whole earth through his Mystical Body, the Church. The disciple will have to make a personal journey and will contribute to continuing the journey of the Church to the ends of the earth.

Other themes—concern and respect for women, the call of all people, not just the Jews, to salvation, the need for faith—also appear in this story.

One of the predominate themes Luke develops is that of discipleship. He begins his Gospel by showing Mary as the perfect disciple, the model for the individual Christian as well as for the entire Church. Mary's great dignity does not lie in the mere fact that she gave birth to the Son of the Most High. It lies in her faith and in her discipleship. She was not a flamboyant disciple like Paul. She did not travel to Rome and die a martyr's death like Peter. She did not write her memories and theological reflections like John. She was a perfectly ordinary person who responded perfectly to the call of God. She was a woman of faith. She received the Savior and followed him. She heard the word of God and acted on it. Therefore Theophilus—and we—can find in her image the pattern of discipleship.

Mary's life depicts the seven stages of discipleship: (1) She received a very unexpected and difficult *call* to be the mother of a unique child in a very strange way. (2) She *tested the call* by asking questions. (3) Without reserve she *accepted* the call. (4) Immediately, without concern for herself, she set off to *help another*, a cousin who was old and in her sixth month of pregnancy. (5) She *shared the Good News* with her cousin. (6) She returned home to give birth and to *show* the child to the shepherds, to the magi, to Simeon and Anna, without fully understanding who he was and what he was all about. (7) She *persevered* to the end, finally standing beneath the cross and burying Jesus.

The events as Luke depicts them sound so miraculous and out of the ordinary that it is easy for us to say, "We can't be like Mary. After all, she is the Mother of the Christ." Yet the pattern is so simple that it can be followed by each of us in daily life.

FOR REFLECTION

People who believe in Jesus the Christ can find the pattern of Mary's life repeating itself in their own efforts to be people of faith. The answers to the questions below most likely will be about some very ordinary event in life—no angel, no big deal, just a call to live according to one of the themes mentioned by Luke.

1) When have you heard a call from God which seemed a bit outlandish or impossible to you?

2) What questions did you ask?

3) Where did you look for help or reassurance?

4) What was your response to the call?

5) What did you do to help another?

6) What did you do to share the Good News?

7) In spite of what difficulties did you persevere?

Taking Up the Cross

Poor Theophilus did not know what he was getting into when he considered becoming a follower of Christ. To be sure, Luke records Jesus telling the apostles, "If anyone wishes to come after me, he must deny himself and take up his cross daily and follow me. For whoever wishes to save his life will lose it, but whoever loses his life for my sake will save it" (9:23-24). When Theophilus received the Gospel it would have been easy for him to see this saying as applying to the extraordinary sufferings endured by those closest to Jesus. Many of the first Christians had had to flee Jerusalem. The first persecution in the year 64 had been bloody but short-lived. All of the apostles but one had died a martyr's death by the year 65. Theophilus may have hoped to be delivered from evil such as that. But if he reflected on the story of Mary, he would have realized that answering the invitation to discipleship always involves suffering.

In the April 1988 issue of *Chicago Studies*, Louis Cameli traces "Mary's experience of suffering presented in the context of faith, hope and love." The Catholic devotion to Mary as the Mother of Sorrows is meant as a comfort for all disciples. It is a mistake to see this devotion as a way to miraculous deliverance from trials and suffering. Whenever our ordinary routine of life is disrupted—especially when we are called to a radical new kind of life—there is an interior struggle with fear and anxiety which involves suffering. And it is the struggle with the suffering which transforms people of faith as they resist the natural tendency to become passive, to give up, to look for easy solutions.

Suffering causes one to become disconnected, at loose ends, confused. Knowing, understanding, accepting—even loving—the situation restores one's connections and brings about transformation. Being concerned about others, getting out of one's self, expanding one's consciousness even in the midst of suffering contributes to the transformation. Giving up control, surrendering to God's will and looking to the future with hope cap the transformation.

FOR REFLECTION

Using Cameli's outline of Mary's sufferings, identify your own suffering, struggles and sorrows. In the Scripture passages listed below, name what you think Mary's fears, worries or sufferings were. Then turn to your own experience.

1) Read Luke 1:26-37, Mary's call.

When you have felt called by God to marry, to have children, to live more in accord with the Gospel, what fears of the unknown, of making a commitment whose consequences are unknown, did you experience?

2) Read Matthew 1:18-25, Joseph's misunderstanding of Mary's situation.

What fear, pain or anxiety about being misunderstood by other people did you feel when you answered God's call?

3) Read Matthew 2:1-18, Herod threatens the life of the child.

What dangers and hostile forces did you face in answering your call? How did you feel about them?

4) *Read Luke 1:22-52, the presentation of Jesus in the temple and his loss there 12 years later.*

What anxiety and worries have you experienced when your call led you into situations which you did not comprehend?

5) *Read Luke 8:19-21, Mary and the relatives of Jesus go to see him.*

When your call has involved breaking ties with family, with friends, with familiar and safe places, what worries and fears have you experienced?

6) *Mary stands at the foot of the cross (John 19:25-30).*

In answering your call, when have you felt worry and concern about the future?

7) *Read John 19:38-42, Mary buries Jesus.*

What suffering have you known when your hopes and plans have apparently failed?

8) *Read Luke 24:36-49, the appearance of Jesus on Easter.*

When you have finally been successful in living up to a particular call, what fears have you still had?

9) *Looking back at your own fears and worries, how have you dealt with them?*

Chapter Two
The Storyteller

WHEN LUKE DIPPED HIS BRUSH into a pot of soot ink and touched the parchment partially unrolled before him, he began a dialogue with Theophilus. He knew his friend. Luke wrote in response to questions, spoken and unspoken— not so much about the *facts* of Jesus' life as about the *meaning* of Jesus and his teachings. Certainly Luke did not know that he would be in a dialogue with us 1,900 years later. Luke wanted to share his own insight, his own experience of Jesus, as well as that of other eyewitnesses.

Luke, a physician, was very sensitive to Jesus' concern for those who were physically ill. As a Gentile, he was conscious of the way Jesus treated Gentiles as well as those whom the Jews considered sinners and outcasts. He also had a deep understanding of the Holy Spirit's activity in the life of Jesus and in the life of the community he left behind. And Luke was perceptive of the good relationships Jesus had with women.

Luke had to use words to record his insights and his experience as faithfully and as fully as possible. More than any other evangelist, he used parables to convey his insights and to answer the questions Theophilus and his friends were asking. We, for our part, have to allow the parables to speak to us today. Luke's parables stand in the place of the visible Jesus to provoke us to reflection about the way we think and act. They challenge our self-understanding and our human values. They call us to unconditional surrender to the Lord.

Our task when we read the stories and sayings in the Gospel is to enter into that dialogue with Luke and discuss the meaning of Jesus. Even though we are separated by two millennia, our common basis for discussion is faith in Jesus. The writer was a man of faith. To understand him we, his readers, need to be believers who accept Jesus' message. From the dialogue we can discover more deeply the meaning of Jesus for our hopes, our expectations, our final fate. That is what Luke is trying to share with us, not the historical details of Jesus' story.

To enter this dialogue it is not enough for us to pick up the book and read. Besides faith, we need the help of scholars to understand Jesus' intentions and the situation in which he spoke. The scholars also have to help us understand Luke's times and intentions, as well as the literary devices he used to communicate what he knew and believed.

We bring to this dialogue our lives, our culture, our 20 centuries of history as Christians. Our dialogue with Luke will therefore be different than that of Roman citizens, Frankish barbarians, medieval theologians and modern Third World people. Yet the purpose of the dialogue is the same: It is to bring peace, joy and purpose to our lives. It is to unite us and to heal the divisions among us. It is to put an end to murder, war, exploitation of any kind. It is to establish peace and justice. It is to help us deepen our identity as members of the people of God, to foster our relationship with Jesus and to foster the unity of sharing a common table. In short, the purpose of this dialogue is reaching for that perfection of love to which each of us is called.

Comparing the Gospels

One special form of dialogue for deepening our understanding of God is the parable. A parable is simply a story with religious meaning drawn from ordinary life. It is intended to challenge the hearer's values and way of looking at life and so bring about a change of heart.

Scholars distinguish three types of parables. Some are about ordinary events which all people have experienced in one way or another, such as the widow's search for a lost coin (Luke 15:8-10). The kingdom of God is compared to these common experiences. Others, such as the story of the sower who went out to sow his seed (Luke 8:5-8), tell a simple story created by Jesus to illustrate a point about the Kingdom. A third kind, such as the parable of the Good Samaritan (Luke 10:30-37), illustrates the way people live in the Kingdom.

Scholars disagree on the exact number of parables in the Gospels. For convenience we will use the list Jan Lambrecht offers in *Once More Astonished*.[2] He lists 42 in the Synoptic Gospels (Matthew, Mark and Luke). Thirty-one of these are found in Luke. Of these 31, nine are also found in Matthew and four in both Matthew and Mark. (See chart on p. 24.) Thus Luke records more parables than Mark and Matthew put together, and 18 are found only in his Gospel.

FOR REFLECTION

1) *To see how parables deal with very ordinary events in people's lives, pick two of the starred parables from the chart on page 24 and think of a common event in your own life which is similar to the incident related by Jesus.*

2) *Think of a point you would like to make to your spouse, your boss or a friend without saying it in so many words. Create a story which makes the point. In what way do you see your story as a challenge to a person's usual way of thinking or acting?*

---

[2]Jan Lambrecht, *Once More Astonished: The Parables of Jesus*, pp. 18-20.

Parables in the Synoptic Gospels

*The Children in the Marketplace	Lk 7:31-35	Mt 11:16-19	
The Two Debtors	Lk 7:41-43		
The Sower	Lk 8:5-8	Mt 13:3-9	Mk 4:3-9
The Good Samaritan	Lk 10:30-37		
*The Persistent Friend	Lk 11:5-8		
The Return of the Evil Spirit	Lk 11:24-26	Mt 12:43-45	
The Rich Fool	Lk 12:16-21		
The Watchful Servants	Lk 12:35-38		
The Burglar at Night	Lk 12:39-40	Mt 24:43-44	
The Faithful or Wicked Servant	Lk 12:42-46	Mt 24:45-51	
Going Before the Judge	Lk 12:58-59	Mt 5:25-26	
The Barren Fig Tree	Lk 13:6-9		
*The Mustard Seed	Lk 13:8-19	Mt 13:31-32	Mk 4:30-32
*The Leaven	Lk 13:20-21	Mt 13:33	
*The Closed Door	Lk 13:24-30		
The Places of Honor	Lk 14: 8-11		
Inviting Guests	Lk 14:12-14		
The Guests Invited to the Feast	Lk 14:16-24	Mt 22:2-14	
*Building a Tower	Lk 14:28-30		
Planning a War	Lk 14:31-32		
The Lost Sheep	Lk 15:4-7	Mt 18:12-14	
*The Lost Coin	Lk 15:8-10		
The Prodigal Son	Lk 15:11-32		
The Unjust Steward	Lk 16:1-8		
The Rich Man and Lazarus	Lk 16:19-21		
The Useless Servant	Lk 17:7-10		
The Unjust Judge	Lk 18:1-8		
The Pharisee and the Publican	Lk 18:9-14		
The Talents/The Pounds	Lk 19:11-27	Mt 25:14-30	
The Wicked Tenants	Lk 20: 9-18	Mt 21:33-44	Mk 12:1-11
The Budding Fig Tree	Lk 21:29-31	Mt 24:32-33	Mk 13:28-29

Elements of a Parable

A parable engages the hearer in dialogue. In our case, since neither the speaker (Jesus) nor the recorder (Luke) is visibly present, we have to dialogue with the text. Because a parable does not lay out its point up front and because it does not always seem to relate to the topic at hand, it forces us to ask, "What's this got to do with what we are talking about? Why did Jesus tell this story? Why did Luke record this story? Why are we talking about it at this time?"

To enter the dialogue we have to know something about the structure of a parable. The story often contains a *surprise*. We read, for example, about a dishonest steward who is to be fired (Luke 16:1-8). He rigs the bills of the boss's debtors so that they will give him a job. We expect the employer to condemn such actions. Instead he does a switch and commends the man's foresight. The ending of the story comes as somewhat of a surprise and causes us to ask Luke, "Why are you telling this story? Why is Jesus talking about such a dishonest man in a complimentary way?"

But when we think about the story for a time *insight* comes. We see that the steward was using the resources he had to take care of him in the future. With a bit of reflection we may realize that this story is also telling us to use the resources we have—money, time, talents—to prepare for our future. Finally, insight calls for a *decision* from us no matter how many times we have heard the story before. Each time we hear it we should be able to see some new application to our lives. Thus the parable contains *surprise*, *insight* and *decision*.

Another way to look at a parable is to see that it spans time. It reveals the *future*; it calls us to break with the *past* and to make a decision in the *present*. Since today's present is different from that of a week, a month or a year ago, a parable always contains a fresh challenge.

1) *Pick any one of the parables in Luke (see chart on page 24) and identify the surprise twist, the insight it gives you about the Kingdom of God or about how its members ought to act and what decision it seems to ask of you.*

2) *Think of yourself as a first-century Jewish man or woman listening to Jesus telling a story about a nobleman who gave his servants varying amounts of gold coins to keep until his return. Read the story (Luke 19:11-17) and then identify how you as that Jewish person might understand what Jesus was saying about the future, the past and the present.*

3) *How does the story speak to your 20th-century self about the future, the present and the past?*

Background of the Parables

The parables are two parts of a three-way conversation, Jesus' and Luke's part of the dialogue. As we read them, we read words which reflect the actual sayings of Jesus *as applied, used and recorded by Luke's community.* We have to supply the third part of that conversation. But to do so we must know something of the context—the time, place, people and situation in which Jesus spoke these words and something of the situation when Luke wrote his words down.

By the time Jesus' words were written down, the circumstances of the lives of his followers had changed. These changes influenced the way they remembered and understood the parables. Today scholars are trying to recover both the setting in which Jesus told a parable and the setting in the early Church which recorded the story. They list many factors which need to be taken into account. Some of the more important of these are:

1) The parables were translated from the original Aramaic which Jesus spoke into Greek, the language in which the Gospels were written, causing subtle changes in meaning.

2) As happens in ordinary conversation, the parables were often embellished as they were retold.

3) Parables originally addressed to the opponents of Jesus or to the crowds who followed him were, in many cases, applied by the primitive Church to the actual situation of the Christian community of a later day. See, for example, the explanation about the sower and the seed in Luke 8:11-15.

FOR REFLECTION

Think of an event in your own life which you have told many times. How have you embellished it, changed it, dropped parts of it or added details or humor to it? What changes can you identify and why do you think you have made them? In what way is the story still true even though you have embellished it?

The Context of the Parables

In reflecting on a parable, we have to take into account both the context in which Jesus spoke it and that in which Luke wrote it if we are to hear the challenge it has for us. Luke was recording the parables not as a Jew hearing them from the lips of Jesus, but as a Christian who had talked about and reflected on them with the other believers.

For example, Luke wrote a story which Jesus told about a man who gave a feast to which the invited guests did not come (Luke 14:1-24). The story follows the accepted etiquette of the time. First the guests received a preparatory invitation which did not give the exact time of the banquet. Then when all was ready the host would send his servants with a second invitation to those who had been invited. Courtesy demanded that those who had been invited and who had presumably accepted should attend. Not to do so was a great offense.

The host is understandably angry when the invited guests all give excuses for not being able to attend. Now the twist: He does a surprising thing. He invites in the poor from the city streets. There is still room so he sends out his servants a second time into the country lanes where foreigners and outcasts live, telling them to bring in all they can find. Thus, the poor, the outcasts and the homeless are compelled to come to the banquet.

Jesus told this story as a rebuke to the critics who refused to listen to him. By the time Luke wrote that was not a big problem for his community. Luke's community was composed of those who had accepted the invitation. Most of those who had been first invited, the Jews, had not accepted Christ. Therefore, Luke uses the parable as a missionary statement indicating that all kinds of people are called to the kingdom. We can see a reference to this intention in the two calls. The first sending forth of the servants was a call to the tax collectors and sinners in Israel; and the second, which came at a later time, a sending forth of the call to the Gentiles.

FOR REFLECTION

1) *Read the story of the Great Feast (Luke 14:15-24). What is the most surprising aspect of this story to you? Where would you put yourself in this parable?*

2) *What insight into the nature of Jesus' message does this parable give you?*

3) *What challenge do you see in this story for the people who heard it from the lips of Jesus?*

4) *In what way was this parable a missionary challenge to the people of Luke's community?*

5) *In what way is it a challenge to our Church today and to us personally?*

Different Uses of the Same Parable

Just because a parable is used one way in one Gospel does not mean that it is used in exactly the same way in another. For example, Matthew 22:1-14 tells the story of the Great Feast with several differences and for a slightly different purpose. His feast is a wedding feast given by a king for his son. The biggest difference is the detail about a man who came in without a wedding garment.

Most commentators think that this was at one time a separate parable which Matthew joined to the one Luke records because he did not want to leave his hearers with the idea that those who were brought to the feast by the servants had no obligation at all. In its missionary activity the Church then and now is confronted with the danger that the doctrine of free grace, of God's unconditional love, frees a person from all moral responsibility. In Matthew's community the wedding garment was a symbol of Baptism—and some people were already being lax in living up to their baptismal commitment. Therefore, Matthew joined the parable of the Wedding Garment to that of the Great Feast. By doing so he introduced the principle of merit and the need for change or repentance if one is to enjoy the eternal banquet.

FOR REFLECTION

1) *Read the two versions of the Great Feast below. Underline words that are changed from one version to the other. Highlight sections that are included in one version but not in the other.*

Luke 14:16-24

[Jesus] replied to him, "A man gave a great dinner to which he invited many. When the time for the dinner came, he dispatched his servant to say to those invited, 'Come, everything is now ready.' But one by one, they all began to excuse themselves. The first said to him, 'I have purchased a field and must go to examine it; I ask you, consider me excused.' And another said, 'I have purchased five yoke of oxen and am on my way to evaluate them; I ask you, consider me excused.' And another said, 'I have just married a woman, and therefore I cannot come.' The servant went and reported this to his master. Then the master of the house in a rage commanded his servant, 'Go out quickly into the streets and alleys of the town and bring in here the poor and the crippled, the blind and the lame.' The servant reported, 'Sir, your orders have been carried out and still there is room.' The master then ordered the servant, 'Go out to the highways and hedgerows and make people come in that my home may be filled. For, I tell you, none of those men who were invited will taste my dinner.' "

Matthew 22:1-14

Jesus again in reply spoke to them in parables, saying, "The kingdom of heaven may be likened to a king who gave a wedding feast for his son. He dispatched his servants to summon the invited guests to the feast, but they refused to come. A second time he sent other servants, saying, 'Tell those invited: "Behold, I have prepared my banquet, my calves and fattened cattle are killed, and everything is ready; come to the feast."' Some ignored the invitation and went away, one to his farm, another to his business. The rest laid hold of his servants, mistreated them, and killed them. The king was enraged and sent his troops, destroyed those murderers, and burned their city. Then he said to his servants, 'The feast is ready, but those who were invited were not worthy to come. Go out, therefore, into the main roads and invite to the feast whomever you find.' The servants went out into the streets and gathered all they found, bad and good alike, and the hall was filled with guests. But when the king came in to meet the guests he saw a man there not dressed in a wedding garment. He said to him, 'My friend, how is it that you came in here without a wedding garment?' But he was reduced to silence. Then the king said to his attendants, 'Bind his hands and feet, and cast him into the darkness outside, where there will be wailing and grinding of teeth.' Many are invited, but few are chosen."

2) *What two things does this chapter suggest you do when you read the parables? What two things does it suggest avoiding?*

3) *What are the most important things you have learned about parables from this chapter?*

Chapter Three
The Healer

THEOPHILUS AND THE COMMUNITY to which he belonged must have asked Luke many questions which arose from their life situation—questions which people still ask today. "What can I do; my life is so badly messed up? What's the use of trying? I'll just fail again. What is the meaning of life?"

People still need encouragement, forgiveness and healing. Because of today's fast pace of life, people have little time to build quality relationships with others. They often feel alienated, separated. They make choices which damage their relationships with others. They experience brokenness and guilt. One author has written, "The earth is a hospital planet," meaning that every person is struggling to overcome some basic limitation. We all need healing from some wound or other. We need assurance that we can be healed.

Luke gives that assurance in the two stories which frame his account of Jesus' ministry of healing and forgiveness. The first depicts Jesus in the synagogue delivering his first sermon (4:14-21). After coming back from dueling with Satan in the desert, Jesus preached to his townsfolk on a passage from Isaiah. He said that he was the one sent "to bring glad tidings to the poor.../to proclaim liberty to captives.../to let the oppressed go free." He announced he was the one "to proclaim a year acceptable to the Lord" (the "year of favor" was a time when all debts were canceled). Jesus was offering forgiveness to all and an opportunity for a new beginning.

The second is his last talk to his followers (24:44-48). Just before he was to return to the Father he told his friends, "Thus it is written that the Messiah would suffer and rise from the dead on the third day and that repentance, for the forgiveness of sins, would be preached in his name to all the nations...." He then commissioned the disciples to take this Good News of forgiveness and a chance to begin again to all the world.

In the incidents framed by these two stories, Jesus the healer brings new life to those he encounters along the way, and Luke assures his friend Theophilus that this new life is available through the Holy Spirit to all those who believe.

In Luke 5:12-26, we find Jesus extending a healing touch to a leper. According to the Jewish law, lepers were to be cut off from the rest of the people: "As long as the sore is on him he shall declare himself unclean, since he is in fact unclean. He shall dwell apart, making his abode outside the camp" (Leviticus 13:46). Jesus reached out to the leper, cured him and restored him to his family and to the community. Thus the man was not only healed of his illness, he was also reinstated into society, healed from alienation and separation.

Then Jesus cures a paralyzed man who had to be lowered through a hole in the roof because the crowd around Jesus was so dense (5:17-26). In this case he first forgives the man's sins and then restores to him the use of his limbs. Both the forgiveness of sins and the healing of disease overcome alienation, loneliness and separation. Jesus cures people so that they can repair and build up their relationships with others and with God.

Luke offers many other examples of Jesus curing and forgiving sins (6:6-11; 7:11-17; 7:36-50; 8:26-39; 9:37-43; 9:49-50). Read one of them. Then complete the following sentences:

1) The story I read was about ———.

2) Before being cured, the person must have felt ———.

3) The person must have experienced separation or alienation from ———.

4) After being cured the person must have felt ———.

5) I think that, after leaving Jesus, the person ———.

6) I can identity with this story because ———.

The Man Who Eats With Sinners

In writing to Theophilus, Luke was trying to convey the kind of person Jesus was. Luke was not only trying to demonstrate Jesus' messiahship; he was also trying to capture the character of Jesus so that the reader could relate to him. He showed that Jesus associated with all kinds of people, rich and poor, socially acceptable people and social outcasts, religious people and sinners. Luke's Jesus, however, favors sinners and the people on the fringes of society. This predilection caused his enemies no little trouble. The self-righteous complained, "This man welcomes sinners and eats with them" (15:2b). Jesus agreed with them: "I have not come to call the righteous to repentance but sinners" (5:32).

This characteristic of Jesus gives hope and reassurance to those who have messed up their lives, to those who feel that they are out of contact with society, to those who are racked by guilt.

1) Describe briefly what you believe sin to be.

2) Which groups of people does the word sinners *bring to your mind?*

3) If Jesus were to come to town today and ask you at which places in town he should preach, what would you suggest to him? Why?

4) From reading the Scriptures, which people or groups of people in your town do you think Jesus would prefer being with? Why?

5) Looking at the way you answered the questions above, how do you feel when you are with the kind of people for whom Jesus had a predilection?

Sin Is Real

Theophilus did not know psychology or the sciences of human behavior; he had no understanding of heredity and environment. His worldview must have been much simpler than ours. These sciences have made it much easier for people today to explain away sin. They have made it much more difficult for people to identify and acknowledge sin in their lives. It is more comforting to relegate responsibility for evil to others—parents, teachers or "those people"—to heredity or to the social system.

But even some who do not want to do away with the idea of sin find it more difficult to recognize it because the concept of sin formed early in their lives is no longer meaningful. They learned the *Baltimore Catechism* definition of actual sin: "any willful thought, word, action or omission forbidden by the law of God." The things that were considered sinful were spelled out in detailed examinations of conscience which listed a wide variety of activities contrary to the Ten Commandments and the precepts of the Church. Though the catechism was careful to stress the need for sufficient knowledge and full consent of the will, most people concentrated on the seriousness of the actions, ignoring the degree of understanding or freedom. They paid little attention to the quality of their life, their attitudes, habits and underlying motivation.

Thus, many people saw sin only in the action itself, abstracted from the totality of their life. This view left untouched a person's real problems and struggles. It did not bring healing where it was most needed: at the deeper level of motivation, responsibility, commitment and conviction.

Since the renewal inaugurated by the Second Vatican Council, the Church has been rethinking the notion of sin. This rethinking has caused confusion for some and for others the attitude that nothing is sin anymore. The renewal is, in fact, an effort to call Catholics to the reality of sin and to the use and misuse of human freedom. It is a call for each of us to take responsibility for our life and our attitudes as well as for our actions.

Luke put the problem very succinctly in the parable of the devious steward and its application (16:1-13). The early Christian community saw in this story a warning about the use of riches. Money is not everlasting, and so one should use wealth to ensure a welcome into eternal dwellings. But they also saw a deep psychological reality in this story. A person cannot devote all his or her energies to two competing values. One cannot serve both God and mammon (money, things, self). The passage indicates a need for a radical choice—either a wholehearted yes to God or a wholehearted yes to things which will perish. There is always the possibility of saying no to God by making something else the center of our lives.

The answers to the questions "What is sin?" and "Where do I need healing?" lie in the answer to another question, "What is the fundamental attitude or motivation in my life?" This question can be asked in any of a number of ways: "Is my life moving in the direction of a deeper union with God and others or is it centering more and more on my own desires and satisfaction?" "Have I, in reality, given my heart to God or to something else?" "Is God the center of my life or is the center something or someone else?"

It may be hard to identify the "master" who is competing for our service because we all like to think that we are basically trying to serve the one God. But most people, even those who sincerely are seeking to serve God, also hear a call for service from other masters. Herein lies the confusion we feel. Herein lies the area which is in need of forgiveness and healing. *Master* is another name for that which gives ultimate meaning or purpose to our life, for that which is the goal of our life, for that on which we set our heart and are willing to sacrifice all else, for that which directs the choices we make. If we examine our lives we will usually find that we have tried to serve various masters at different times in our lives.

FOR REFLECTION

1) *Cite one or two popular phrases which echo Jesus' words, "No servant can serve two masters. Either he will hate one and love the other, or be devoted to one and despise the other. You cannot serve God and mammon" (Luke 16:13).*

2) *What are some of the "masters" you have seen people trying to serve?*

3) *What have you seen happen in the lives of people who have tried to serve two masters?*

4) *In your efforts to follow Jesus, with what would-be masters do you contend?*

Sin: The Absence of Love

The call of the Christian life is a call to give one's heart fully and completely to God, to love God and others. "You shall love the Lord, your God, with all your heart, with all your soul and with all your mind....[Y]ou shall love your neighbor as yourself" (Matthew 22:37b, 39b). Sin is breaking or rupturing this love relationship with God and others. Far more than simply breaking a law, sin is something which proceeds from the very heart of a person. It is withdrawing oneself from God and from others, turning away from the Creator of life to embrace something created. This created reality, in turn, can become the god of one's life.

FOR REFLECTION

1) *St. John said that God is love (see 1 John 4:7-16). Jesus said we are to love even our enemies (Luke 6:27-28). St. Paul describes love in soaring words in his First Letter to the Corinthians (13:4-7). By looking for some of these qualities in our relationship with people we do not like, we will be able to begin to plumb our love for God. Someone has said that the measure of our love for God is the measure of our love for the person we like least.*

Take a moment to think of a person you love very little or not at all.

On a scale of 1 to 10 (10 being highest, 1 being not at all), rate the way you treat this person in the areas mentioned by Paul in 1 Corinthians 13:4-7:

___*patient*	___*forgiving injuries*
___*kind*	___*compassionate*
___*understanding*	___*believing good about others*
___*seeking others' interests*	___*hope-filled*
___*even-tempered*	___*constant*

2) *What do your answers suggest to you about the quality of your love for God?*

3) *What do your answers suggest to you about ways you might grow in loving God?*

The Need for Forgiveness

Reading Scripture is a call to face reality—to see how we may be trying to serve two masters, to see how we may be failing in love, to see that we may have bad attitudes and bad habits, to see that we do make wrong choices. Reflecting on Scripture helps us realize that sin is a reality in our lives and that each of us needs forgiveness. It may be hard to admit that something is wrong deep in our lives, but the sad fact is that all people need Christ's forgiveness to grow in union with God and neighbor.

The process of forgiveness and restoration may take time and effort to complete but it is relatively simple. The phases of the process flow in this order:

1) *Sin:* the attitude or event which breaks the relationship with God and neighbor. It begins with the attitude, for the action is an expression of the evil intention in a person's heart.

2) *Recognition of sin:* acknowledging that one's choice has taken one far from God and that one is guilty.

3) *Expressing sorrow:* changing one's life, seeking forgiveness and expressing sorrow to the Father or to Jesus.

4) *God's response:* forgiveness and instantaneous restoration of the relationship, no questions asked.

5) *New way of life:* a different kind of life, one of union with God and fellowship with others.

1) Luke illustrates this five-step process most clearly in the story of the Prodigal Son (15:11-32). Briefly identify and describe each step of the process in the story.

2) Which of these steps do you ordinarily find the most difficult? Why?

Social Sin

Sin affects our relationship not only with God but also with others. It is the opposite of love. Love has been described as "being for another." Love unites; love shows concern and care for others. Love is giving one's life for another's best interests.

Sin, on the other hand, places our own interests first. It does not seek the best interests of the other. It is destructive of a relationship because it deprives another of the gift of ourself and of the love God intends to share through us. But sin as a refusal to love has a greater effect than to harm or break a relationship with an individual. Most often it joins with the sins and the refusals to love of others and creates a climate of social disorder which in turn oppresses the weak, the poor and the disadvantaged.

Take, for example, the way Hitler was able to play on his people's anti-Semitic bias until it escalated into the Holocaust. Some of his compatriots shared his hatred of the Jews and were eager to take part in their oppression. Others held no prejudice but still failed to act in a loving way; keeping silence out of fear or a sense that it was none of their business, they permitted the evil to grow until six million Jews perished in the death camps.

1) Find a picture in a magazine which illustrates a social or collective sin. In what ways do many people contribute to this sin?

2) List four or five ways the collective sins of many people affect daily life, causing what we call "social problems."

3) How do those who are not actively contributing to the problem affect the issue for better or for worse?

4) What do you think a person might do to seek healing for his or her role in the collective sins of humankind?

Continuing to Proclaim Forgiveness

Zacchaeus the tax collector (Luke 19:1-10), the woman taken in adultery (John 8:1-11) and the good thief (Luke 23:39-43) were personally forgiven and healed by Jesus. After Jesus ascended into heaven, the community he left behind, his Mystical Body, continued to call sinners to a change of heart by announcing the Good News of the forgiveness of sins. This announcement has taken many forms in the course of the history of the Christian community, but each form has required not merely an interior acknowledgement of sin and sorrow but also an external sign of the forgiveness granted by God. For example, Baptism is seen as a response to a Gospel call and a way of forgiveness. The Anointing of the Sick is a sign of Christ's forgiveness and healing power. The Eucharist proclaims the death of Jesus as a saving death, a forgiving death, a healing death, until he comes again.

In the Catholic Church healing from sin has been especially associated with the Sacrament of Reconciliation. In the first centuries it was assumed that when one was baptized one had repented and changed one's life. But human nature being what it is, people did not always live up to their commitment. They sinned and were in need of forgiveness and reconciliation.

Prayers, good works and participation in the Eucharist along with sorrow were seen as sufficient for garden-variety sinfulness. Certain sins—murder, open adultery and apostasy—were viewed as so serious that more was required. The person had to confess to the bishop, do public penance to demonstrate a change in way of life and then be publicly readmitted to the congregation on Holy Thursday. Although an argument raged for two centuries over whether a person could be admitted to reconciliation more than once in a lifetime, the basic elements of what is popularly called confession can be found in this practice.

The practice changed as times changed. When it was no longer so dangerous to be a Christian and when people were baptized for less worthy motives ("Be baptized or have your head chopped off!"), Baptism was not so clear a sign of change of life and embracing Christ. More sins were added to the list requiring public reconciliation. Other practices developed: confessing not only to the bishop but to any priest, confessing lesser or venial sins as well as more serious ones, confessing frequently instead of just once in a lifetime. Tracing the history of these changes is fascinating. All the time the five basic steps of the process of forgiveness (see page 40) were present in some way, with different emphases at different times.

The reforms of the Second Vatican Council reflect the bishops' concern to make the Sacrament of Reconciliation echo more clearly the biblical call to acknowledge sin, repent, turn to God, receive forgiveness and change one's life. The penitent is invited to talk about the deep attitudes and habits that prevent surrendering completely to God and a life of loving service. In addition to listing actions contrary to the Commandments and Church law, penitents are challenged to look at their attitudes, habits and values and answer questions such as "How well am I living the Christian life? How am I growing in love for God and neighbor?"

Chapter Four

The Living Lord

THE FOUR EVANGELISTS ALL TOLD the same story but in slightly different ways. The bishops at Vatican Council II explained the differences in these words:

> The sacred authors wrote the four Gospels, selecting some things from among the many which had been handed on by word of mouth or in writing, reducing some of them to a synthesis, explicating some things in view of the situation of their churches, and preserving the form of the proclamation but always in such fashion that they told us the honest truth about Jesus.
> (*Constitution on Divine Revelation*, #19)

The words of the bishops summarize years of scholarly study and hundreds of books about how and why the authors of the various books of Scripture were written as they were.

FOR REFLECTION

1) *Before going any further, reread the bishops' words above. Rewrite the paragraph in your own words to make sure you understand the importance of what the bishops wrote.*

2) *What implications do you think this paragraph has for the way we read the Gospels?*

Selective Hearing

Facile interpretations of the events in Jesus' life tend to be simplistic. They miss the deeper and more subtle meanings in the events. Understanding and interpreting a Scripture story is so much more complex than it appears at first. Besides all the questions about the original meaning of words, about the historical context of events or sermons, about the purpose of the author and about the literary form used, there is the question of the receptivity of the hearer or reader.

People often hear only what they want to hear. Their minds speed down one track, and they do not or cannot see that there are tracks going in other directions. Education, culture, history and personal experience all contribute to this myopic reading of the Scriptures. In addition to this predetermined mindset, people tend to catch only bits and snatches of a Gospel reading because their minds drift or they become distracted and think of something else.

FOR REFLECTION

To see how this process of selective hearing occurs try this activity. (If you are reading this book alone, ask a few friends to do it with you.)

1) *Read Luke 24:13-35 and, without discussion, write a 20-word synopsis of the story. Have each person share with the others what he or she wrote.*

2) *Have one person reread the story out loud while the others note what they added or omitted.*

3) *Discuss whether the omissions or additions gave a different flavor to the story and why they may have been made.*

This process of selective hearing and recalling information is normal. It is so normal that a great percentage of the disagreements arising between people come from the fact that one has not heard fully what the other is saying. When we become conscious of the process, however, we can go back more carefully to the original statements to catch more of their intended meaning. In fact, we may have to go back many times to what was said or written before we can have a clear understanding of what was being communicated. Each time we may see something different. And other people may see things which we did not see or hear. This is particularly true of the Gospels.

FOR REFLECTION

Return to the story of the two disciples on the way to Emmaus. Now that you have heard it or read it twice, what do you think Luke was trying to tell his community of first- or second-generation Christians?

The Faith Journey

We may not be sure exactly why Luke included the story of the two disciples' trip to Emmaus in his Gospel, but we can identify in it five things the two disciples did as they developed their relationship with Christ and with his community of disciples, the Church. In that short walk from Jerusalem to Emmaus, they experienced all five essential characteristics of the Christian faith journey. No one of these characteristics can be omitted if one is to experience the fullness of Christian life:

1) The journey is made with others, in community.
2) The journey involves sharing life, especially faith, expectations and experiences.

3) Understanding of the meaning of these experiences and expectations comes from studying the Scriptures.

4) Recognizing the presence of Jesus on the journey comes from prayer and the celebration of the Eucharist.

5) The journey does not end with recognition of Jesus. It also requires sharing in word and deed the Good News of his resurrection.

FOR REFLECTION

Reread the story (Luke 24:13-35) and pick out a word, phrase or sentence which illustrates each of these steps.

Phases of the Journey

As they sauntered along that road, those two perplexed disciples also made an inner journey which fell into five phases. These phases are the same that all Christians experience in one way or another as they develop their relationship with Christ and his community of disciples, the Church: (1) initial discovery of Jesus; (2) disillusionment or loss of Jesus; (3) rebuilding the relationship; (4) rediscovery of Jesus; (5) mission. This pattern does not occur just once. It is repeated many times in our lives.

The first phase is *the initial discovery of Jesus*, that time when a person discovers that Jesus is important in one's life, that he has the answers to one's questions and that he is the fulfillment of one's expectations. For the two disciples it was the discovery of Jesus in Galilee. They saw him as the one who would set Israel free. He gave new meaning to their lives. Their old way of living was no longer satisfying. In their excitement they heard his call, "Follow me." They left the fishing or the farming or the shop work to someone else, left all and followed him.

48

Your initial enthusiastic discovery of the Lord may have been your childhood experience of Jesus or your initial strong attraction to him as an adult. It was a time when you thought you knew the Lord and walked with him. Describe briefly when that time was, what you thought and felt about Jesus, what you expected from him and some of the activities that demonstrated your relationship with him.

Phase two is *the loss or disillusionment* which occurs when one feels that Christ has let one down because one's hopes and expectations have not been met. For the two disciples it was the crucifixion of Jesus in Jerusalem. They had left everything to follow him and he did not live up to their expectations as the Messiah. They lost faith in what he had said and done. In addition, they lost faith in themselves and in the community. They realized that one of them had betrayed him, others had denied him and most had abandoned him.

In short, they lost their vision; life no longer had any meaning or purpose. Things had not turned out the way they had planned. Jesus was no more. He was dead. Just as the Israelites after the Exodus doubted God's presence among them and cried, "Is the LORD in our midst or not?" (Exodus 17:7b), the two disciples also despaired and groaned, "But we were hoping that he would be the one to redeem Israel..." (Luke 24:21a).

Think about a time when you lost touch with the Lord. How did this loss come about? What other things were going on in your life at the time? How did you feel about life, about losing the Lord? Did your religious behavior change? If so, how?

The third phase, *rebuilding the relationship with Jesus,* can be long and painful. It often occurs in very unexpected ways as the result of encountering unexpected people or events. The two disciples faced the emptiness brought on by their loss of Jesus and shared it with one another. Even though they did not recognize it at the time, this sharing became the basis for new life, for a new and different relationship with Christ and the community.

During this time the Lord's presence was not evident even though it was part of the process of coming to a new and deeper faith. "[T]hey were conversing about all the things that had occurred....Jesus himself drew near and walked with them, but their eyes were prevented from recognizing him...." (Luke 24:15-16). With this stranger they shared the facts of the last few days. They shared their hopes and expectations. They shared what others had said and how others interpreted these same events.

The stranger, who did not seem to know what it was all about, challenged them. "Oh, how foolish you are! How slow of heart to believe all that the prophets spoke!" (24:25b). Then he began with the prophets and explained what had to happen. Later they reflected on the journey and declared, "Were not our hearts burning [within us] while he spoke to us on the way and opened the scriptures to us?" (24:32b).

Sharing, being open to the unexpected, studying the Scriptures and a prayer of longing always are part of the rebuilding process. For the disciples, the rebuilding phase ended when they invited the stranger to stay with them. This was a prayer, an expression of longing for more of the stranger's presence. Jesus quickly and graciously answered their request.

FOR REFLECTION

Recall your efforts and the events which helped you get in touch with Jesus once more. What restrained you from

*recognizing him? Who were the people with whom you
shared and who helped you rebuild the relationship? What
role did the reading of Scripture, prayer and liturgy play
in rebuilding your relationship with Jesus?*

Phase Four, *rediscovery*, depends on the action of Jesus. He
responded to the disciples' plea to stay with them. He took
the bread, blessed it, broke it and gave it to them. In a flash
they recognized that he was present in the broken bread.
Jesus was alive! He was present! All he had said was true!

"The breaking of the bread" was the early Church's
term for the Eucharist, which was central to the disciples'
rediscovery of the risen Jesus. At this point their lives
suddenly had new meaning, new purpose. This Jesus who
had been their teacher and friend, who had died on a cross,
was much more than they had ever expected. They
recognized him as Lord, for the king and Messiah he truly is.
They had a new and deeper relationship with him. He had
vanished from their sight only to make his presence known
time and time again as they retold their story and broke
bread in memory of him.

In the rediscovery phase of our journey it is necessary
to become acutely aware of the Lord's presence not only in
his story, the Gospels, but also in the Eucharist, where he
gives himself to us as food for the journey.

FOR REFLECTION

*Reflect on whether you feel that you have rediscovered
Jesus yet. If you have, how do you feel about him? In the
process of rediscovery what have you learned about Jesus?
About yourself? What part has the Eucharist played in
this process? If you have not rediscovered him, how do you
feel about that? What do you think is hindering you?*

The fifth phase is *mission*. With their discovery of the risen Jesus, the two disciples realized that they had been given a mission to share the Good News with others. They could not keep it to themselves. "So they set out at once and returned to Jerusalem..." (24:33a).

It is interesting that they went back to where they had come from. They did not go to new places. They went back to the people they knew as new people with a new message, "The Lord is risen!" They recounted what had happened on the road and how they had come to know him in the breaking of the bread. The mission they had was part of the mission of the community, the Church, the new People of God. It is in this community, which still exists for our benefit, that lives are shared, Jesus' presence felt, the Scriptures explained, bread is broken and the Good News proclaimed today.

FOR REFLECTION

1) Describe briefly a time when you rediscovered Jesus.

2) How have your thinking, your feelings and your activities changed as a result of your rediscovery of Jesus?

3) What do you do to share the Good News with those who do not know Jesus, those who are suffering physically and mentally, those in despair and doubt?

4) What does this story tell you about the relative importance of breaking open the Scriptures and the breaking of the bread?

5) In what way is the breaking of bread on Sunday a revelation of Jesus' presence for you?

6) In light of this story, what would you tell someone who calls himself or herself Christian but very seldom participates in the breaking of bread?

Chapter Five
Table Fellowship

L UKE NOT ONLY TOLD THEOPHILUS about the process of getting a better understanding and a deeper relationship with Jesus, he also painted pictures for him, each of which illustrated qualities to be found in one who is sincerely seeking to walk in the way of the Lord. He not only used the sayings of Jesus to demonstrate the qualities of discipleship, he also told stories about the many meals Jesus had. In these stories we can find those qualities which should be evident in the disciple who wants to sit in table fellowship with Jesus and the community.

Eating together was an essential characteristic of Luke's Christian community. The sharing of bread and wine blessed in memory of Jesus might not yet have been separated from a common meal. It certainly was not the ritualized ceremony that it would become within a century or two. But Luke's community knew that somehow their identity as Christians, their vision of what makes life worthwhile, their character as people of faith centered on and depended on their table fellowship.

Those first Christians were no different than we are today in the 20th century. Their belief in Jesus did not magically transform their likes and dislikes, their values. In fact, one of the purposes of gathering around the table of the Lord was to explore and judge their personal values as well as the values of the society in which they lived in light of the values they saw in the preaching and actions of Jesus.

These values are admirably summed up in Luke's meal stories. There are nine of them in the Gospel and one in Acts:

1) Levi's party (5:27-39);

2) Dinner with Simon the Pharisee (7:36-50);

3) The feeding of the multitude (9:10-17);

4) Dinner with Martha and Mary (10:38-42);

5) Dinner at a Pharisee's home (11:37-54);

6) Dinner with another Pharisee (14:1-24);

7) Dinner with Zacchaeus (19:1-10);

8) The Last Supper (22:14-38);

9) The meal at Emmaus (24:13-15);

10) Table-fellowship in the early Christian community (Acts 2:44-47).

These stories are like great heroic paintings hung around a banquet hall, each portraying one aspect of the vision and the kind of actions which mold a Christian character.

One of the problems we have today is relating our present experience to that of Luke's first-century community. The way the Mass is celebrated today makes it difficult for us to think of it as a meal or a banquet: We are silent instead of chatting. We sit in pews instead of at a table. There are no plates or silverware in front of us. The bread looks like a piece of round cardboard, and there is no meat or potatoes.

Nevertheless, our present form of the Eucharist evolved from a meal. We need to keep this fact in mind as we look at the meal pictures in Luke so that we can appreciate what these pictures say about the kind of people we are called to be.

As we stroll around the banquet hall and look at Luke's paintings, you will have opportunities to ask yourself, "When I come to the Eucharist, to what degree have I adopted the values Luke has so vividly portrayed in this

meal story?" But first explore your own concepts of
Eucharist.

FOR REFLECTION

1) *What do you think you are doing when you participate
in the Mass?*

2) *What are your reasons for going to Mass?*

3) *To what degree do you feel at one with the other people
who celebrate the Eucharist with you?*

4) *What do you usually get out of Mass?*

Beginning at the End

We will look at Luke's meal stories from back to front:
beginning at the end and working backward. Our
beginning—Luke's end—is in his sequel to the Gospel, the
Acts of the Apostles, where he paints an idyllic picture of the
post-Resurrection Christian community:

> All who believed were together and had all things in
> common; they would sell their property and
> possessions and divide them among all according to
> each one's needs. Every day they devoted themselves
> to meeting together in the temple area and to breaking
> bread in their homes. They ate their meals with
> exultation and sincerity of heart, praising God and
> enjoying favor with all the people. And every day the
> Lord added to their number those who were being
> saved. (Acts 2:44-47)

These were people in the first flush of excitement and
enthusiasm at the Resurrection. Something wonderful had
happened for them and to them. With great vigor they tried
to live the kind of life Jesus had laid out for them. They cared

57

for and shared with one another. They prayed daily and recalled the memory of Jesus in the breaking of bread. Their hearts throbbed with joy, peace and sincerity, and they drew others into their fellowship.

How long this enthusiasm lasted and whether all believers really lived this way are questions which we cannot answer today. Luke, writing 50 years after Pentecost, may have seen those first years through rose-colored glasses. In any case, Paul's letters, written 20 or 30 years earlier, reflect a different picture. Not all Christians were as enthusiastic, sincere and pious as Luke pictures them.

Luke nevertheless depicted an *ideal* succeeding generations could strive for. His meal stories fill out this ideal. Today we can look at each of these stories and ask ourselves to what degree our actions show that we have bought into the attitudes and values pictured by Luke.

FOR REFLECTION

Reflect on your experience of the Christian community. When has it been closest to Luke's ideal? When has it been most distant from that norm?

The Meal at Emmaus (24:13-15)

In Chapter Four we looked at the Emmaus story as a model for discipleship. Here we narrow our focus to the meal itself. Three people are sitting at a simple table. Before the meal is finished, two disciples are totally convinced that Jesus has risen from the dead and is alive after they had felt that they had lost contact with him when he was crucified.

A good many Catholics today feel that they have lost touch with Christ. The sacraments and practices of their youth no longer serve them well. Yet they still feel a need to find Jesus, or at least to have a closer personal relationship with him. Reflection and study groups, Bible circles and the cry for better homilies are signs of this hunger.

When we look at the picture of three people sharing bread and wine in a country inn two thousand years ago, we may well ask what that picture says to the doubt, the despair, the hunger of today. The disciples had been torn by doubts and despair. They had lost hope; they had given up; they were on their way home disillusioned by the events of the previous three days. In the turmoil of modern life each of us can surely identify with their feelings of doubt, despair and confusion.

The third, a stranger, had been talking to them of the Scriptures. Now they were eating their evening meal—and suddenly the stranger's identity was obvious.

FOR REFLECTION

1) *At the Eucharist we proclaim, "Christ has died, Christ is risen, Christ will come again." What doubts or questions about Jesus, his resurrection or his return do you have?*

2) *How do you feel about having these doubts and questions? How do you deal with them?*

3) *How often do you share your doubts and feeling with others? Where do you look for help with them?*

The two disciples journeying from Jerusalem to Emmaus were sharing reflections on their doubts and feelings about the events which had occurred in the past three days. This reflection, this questioning, did not in itself dispel their feelings of despair. It did, however, cause them to be willing to talk to a stranger about their feelings. He in turn explained to them how the Scriptures bore witness to the risen Christ. Even though their hearts burned when he interpreted the

Scriptures for them and they grasped the meaning of what he said, they did not recognize the risen Christ.

Today any number of Catholics are turning to Bible Churches and preachers to find Christ. They miss the conclusion of Luke's story. The exposition of the Scriptures is necessary to turn the soil, to prepare the way, to open the heart, to give hope that the risen Christ is alive and present. But only when they broke bread and shared wine with Jesus did they recognize the risen Christ. It is the Eucharist which reveals the risen Lord's presence to his followers.

This revelation is not automatic. It comes only when believers have the attitudes of the two disciples. The two travelers were open about their doubts and their hopes. They listened and were open to a different interpretation of Scripture than they were used to hearing. They were open to the stranger, willing to sit at the same table with him and share what they had with him.

FOR REFLECTION

1) *What quality did the two disciples manifest in sharing their feelings and thoughts with the stranger?*

2) *What helpful or disappointing experiences of sharing hopes, dreams, expectations and disappointments with someone have you had?*

3) *What do you usually do during the week (reflection, reading Scripture, prayer) to prepare for celebrating the Sunday Eucharist?*

Most of us experience conflicting emotions when we attend Mass. We want the service to have meaning. We want to believe that what we are doing is important for our lives, that what we have been told about the Eucharist is true. Yet our senses give us no evidence. We are not at the foot of the cross

60

or at the Last Supper. We do not see the risen Lord. Doubt, questions, confusion sometimes challenge everything that we have been told is the Good News.

When the two disciples got back to Jerusalem this was the condition of the apostles and the others gathered in the upper room. All had heard of the Resurrection. They wanted it to be true, but their common sense told them something different. Yet Peter, the two disciples and some of the women all said that they had seen Jesus.

Suddenly he was there in their midst, offering them his greatest gift, peace. His presence was meant to bring peace to troubled minds, peace to fearful people, peace to those tormented by doubts. When the apostles still could not believe their eyes and so could not accept his gift, he urged them to touch him and look at the holes in his hands and feet. They were amazed and joyful but still incredulous. So Jesus did what he had done so many times when he had something important to say or do: He asked for food.

They gave him a fish, a snack rather than a meal. He ate, thus proving he was alive and real, not a ghost. Later Peter presented the fact of eating with Jesus as proof of the resurrection. "This man God raised [on] the third day and granted that he be visible...to us...who ate and drank with him after he rose from the dead" (Acts 10:40).

Once conviction seeped deep into their consciousness, those in that room were ready to hear the promise that they would receive power from on high to go forth and preach. They were to announce the Good News about a loving God who forgives sins and who calls all people to live in peace and harmony and community.

From this story we can see that eating with the risen Lord is meant to have a double effect on those who believe: (1) It brings them peace and conviction. The doubts, questions, even turmoil they may feel give way to peace because Christ has achieved victory over all the forces that possibly could overwhelm them. (2) It turns their gaze to other people because conviction and peace are not meant to be clutched to one's bosom. They are meant to be shared with others who are burdened with guilt, with fear, with doubt, with loneliness.

These two consequences of sharing in the Eucharist have been embedded in the prayers of the Mass. Time and time again they ask for peace, for conviction, for strength to share with others.

FOR REFLECTION

Next time you go to Mass, listen carefully to the prayers to see how often these basic ideas are mentioned in one way or another. Before you go to Mass it would also help to ask yourself questions such as these:

1) *When have you found that sharing in the liturgy has brought you peace? How did you feel and what did you do as a result of having that peace?*

2) *How do you feel about giving and receiving the sign of peace at Mass?*

3) *How has the experience of sharing your faith in the risen Lord with another person deepened your faith?*

The Farewell Banquet (Luke 22:14-38)

The story of the Last Supper is retold at every Eucharist—the action of people who remember, people who see the past as vitally important to their present.

Memories give context and meaning to everything that happens to us. Good, bad, indifferent, exciting, peaceful, loving, hateful—they all combine to help us know who and what we are. People who have lost their memories or even part of their memories do not know where they came from, how they relate to other people, what has been important in their lives.

The two disciples who went to Emmaus were talking about their memories. Perhaps they had been present at Jesus' farewell banquet on the night before he died. If they hadn't, they certainly must have heard about that banquet and what Jesus said at it before they had set out for home. Surely they recalled other meals they had shared with Jesus. These memories helped them understand what the stranger was doing when he blessed bread and shared it with them.

We are not sure exactly what Jesus said at the Last Supper. The Gospels differ in the words they record. In writing about that farewell dinner, Luke drew upon the liturgical formulas which his community used when it gathered to celebrate the Lord's Supper: "Jesus took bread, gave thanks, broke the bread and gave it to his disciples."

FOR REFLECTION

1) *What important events in your life do you associate with eucharistic celebrations?*

2) *What memories do you have of eucharistic celebrations that moved you deeply?*

3) *What memories do you have of Masses that bored you or even turned you off?*

4) *How have those celebrations affected subsequent celebrations of the Eucharist?*

We gather for the Eucharist to remember because Jesus said, "Do this in memory of me." Remembering is what the little group gathered in the upper room were doing. They were celebrating the Passover, a feast celebrated "in remembrance." This feast calls the Jews to remember how God freed them from slavery in Egypt. Moreover, it calls upon *God* to remember leading God's people out of slavery into freedom in the promised land. Whenever God and the people together remember the Exodus, the people, just like those in Moses' time, experience the freeing action of God. The Jews believe that God does what God recalls.

Today when we celebrate the Eucharist in memory of Jesus we are calling upon God to remember saving us through the death, resurrection and glorification of Jesus. We believe that salvation is made present to us, is happening for us here and now. In this sense the Mass is the sacrifice of the cross repeated here and now. God and we are remembering in a special way the key events in Jesus' life: his death, resurrection, ascension and eventual return.

The memories recalled at Mass are more than an account of the Last Supper or of Calvary. They are memories of all the meals Jesus had with his friends. They are memories of what he said and did at these various meals so that we can appreciate more what kind of people we are being called to be.

FOR REFLECTION

1) *At Mass, what events from the life of Christ usually come to your memory?*

2) *In the various Eucharistic Prayers the Church outlines the evidences of God's power and concern which we are called to remember. What two or three important saving events have you heard mentioned in the Eucharistic Prayer?*

We associate many powerful memories with the Last Supper: Judas' betrayal, the washing of the feet, the long and moving talk by Jesus. But the occasion itself speaks to us of freedom, of liberation. We all long to be free of the individual kind of slavery we experience, just as the apostles longed to be free from Roman oppression. At this Last Supper Jesus was assuring his friends that what he was doing and what he would do the next day was the most freeing event the world would ever experience.

We see a group of people gathered in an upper room, a guest chamber. This was the home of a friend, not one of their own homes. Because the Passover meal had to be eaten within the walls of Jerusalem, every household in the city was obliged to put any extra rooms at the disposal of the pilgrims who thronged into the city at Passover. In return for this hospitality, the owner of the house received the skin of the lamb slain in sacrifice in the Temple. We see Jesus and his companions in such a guest room, carpeted with rugs. They recline on couches spaced around a low table because the Passover meal celebrated the Israelites' becoming a free people. Only the free ate reclining. Slaves ate standing or sitting on stools.

The slavery Jesus frees us from is sin, and sin has its basis in fear: fear of dying because we have no hope of an afterlife, fear of rejection because we think that we are not lovable to God, fear of failure because we know we are so weak in the face of temptations, fear of the suffering which we know must be our lot if we are to enter the Kingdom. Jesus by his own death faced all these fears and overcame them. He assures us by giving us himself as our food that we too can overcome them. We stand and sit and kneel at the Eucharist as a sign that we are people who have been freed, but each of us has to accept that freedom and live it.

FOR REFLECTION

We usually look at the things outside ourselves which make our lives difficult, but as we look at the scene of the Last Supper we should ask ourselves what is within us, what fears enslave us.

1) What is your greatest fear at the present time?

2) How do you see the fear of rejection by others, the fear of

*failure and suffering or the fear of death, either physical
or psychological, operating in your life?*

3) *When you participate in the liturgy with fear in your
life, what message of the memory of Jesus calms your
fear?*

Memories help us know who we are, but we must also look
to the future in order to have hope for what we might be and
for what might happen. The Christian vision has a strong
note of hope in it, a trust that the Lord will come at some time
to set right all that is wrong. At the Supper Jesus looked to
the future when, after a terrible time, he would once again
eat and drink with his friends in the Kingdom of God. But
now Jesus adds a note for the future, a time when he will
return and bring the fullness of that Kingdom into human
history.

The idea of the Second Coming may not have much
impact on our lives. The two disciples may well have felt that
since they saw Jesus and ate with him, the great messianic
Kingdom in all its power and glory had arrived. But by the
time Luke wrote there were few signs that Christ was about
to appear at any minute. The first persecutions had hit the
community in Rome and in other spots in the empire. The
Christians had been expelled from the Jewish synagogues.
Heresies were dividing the community. Those early
Christians took the notion of the Second Coming very
literally, but they must have experienced great
disappointment as the years went on and Jesus did not
return in the way they expected him to.

Few of us think that the Second Coming will occur in
our lifetime. But we do believe that through the Eucharist
Jesus does come again among his followers. As the Fathers of
Vatican Council II wrote:

> At the Last Supper, on the night when He was betrayed, our Savior instituted the Eucharistic Sacrifice of His Body and Blood. He did this in order to perpetuate the sacrifice of the Cross throughout the centuries until He should come again, and so to entrust to His beloved spouse, the Church, a memorial of His death and resurrection: a sacrament of love, a sign of unity, a bond of charity, a paschal banquet in which Christ is consumed, the mind is filled with grace, and a pledge of future glory is given us. (*Constitution on the Sacred Liturgy,* #47)

Christ comes giving us the hope that we can become better people, that we can be united and be servants of one another as he prayed for us to be. He comes with the trust and hope that the Church will not fail, that it will spread the Good News of brotherhood, peace and forgiveness. As we stand in the present and remember the past, we are called to be a people of hope who trust that the Holy Spirit will guide the Church through the agonizing struggle of change as it tries to bring the Kingdom of God into reality in the hearts of people.

FOR REFLECTION

1) What do you believe the Second Coming of Jesus means?

2) How does this belief affect the way you see life?

3) How does this belief affect the way you act?

4) If you knew Jesus Christ were coming again tomorrow, what would you do?

Of course, we cannot look at a picture of the farewell banquet without hearing the Lord's words, "This is my body which will be given for you....This cup is the new covenant in my blood, which will be shed for you" (Luke 22:19b,20b). These words are a tremendous challenge to our faith. The vision they hold out is the reality of Christ's presence.

This image has been accepted by the Catholic and Orthodox traditions for two thousand years and in a different way by many in the Protestant tradition. How that presence comes about has troubled Christians ever since they began to ask "How?" along with the questions "What?" and "Who?" These words, so clear in the Scripture and uttered every day at the altar, ask us to what degree we believe that Jesus has risen and is alive, the same yet different, present with us.

Our answer can be purely notional. We accept the idea because we have been told it is so, but it has little or no effect upon our lives. Or it can be operational, a driving force in all we say and do.

FOR REFLECTION

1) *When you eat the bread and/or drink of the cup of Eucharist, which of the following statements comes closest to what you actually believe?*

—*That bread and wine are actually the risen Christ.*

—*That bread and wine are only a symbol or sign of the presence of Jesus.*

—*That bread and wine remain the same but now have a spiritual and mystical meaning.*

—*Something else. (If so, what?)*

2) *The* Baltimore Catechism *expressed Catholic belief this way: The bread and wine become the body and blood, soul and divinity of Jesus. In other words they become Christ. If this belief really were more than words, a motivating force in believers' lives, how do you think it would affect the way they live, deal with other people and pray?*

Supper With a Tax Collector (Luke 19:1-10)

One of the most moving pictures Luke paints is that of a short man standing before Jesus in a stance of welcome and saying, "Behold, half of my possessions, Lord, I shall give to the poor, and if I have extorted anything from anyone I shall repay it four times over" (Luke 19:8). A rich man has just uttered the words which are his passport to enter the Kingdom.

Well-off, middle-class Americans are often disturbed by the call to follow the poor Jesus. In the Gospel he and his band of followers look very much like street people who have no home and who accept food and shelter wherever they can find them. This discomfort is increased by the story of the official who turned down Jesus' offer of discipleship and went away sad because he could not sell all and give it to the poor (Luke 18:18-23). It is heightened still further when Jesus comments that "it is easier for a camel to pass through the eye of a needle than for a rich person to enter the kingdom of God" (Luke 18:25). But then Luke gives a reassuring picture of a well-off man in the town of Jericho who did enter the Kingdom.

Jericho, situated in the rich Jordan valley about six miles north of the Dead Sea, was on an important trade route between Judea and Perea. Duty was collected on all merchandise going between the two provinces. The right to collect these tolls was auctioned off by the Romans to the highest bidder. This chief tax collector often collected more than was lawful and became wealthy on the difference between what his agents collected and what he paid the Romans. The Jews despised him for working for the Romans and for gouging his own people.

Luke pictures such a wealthy tax collector, Zacchaeus, who wanted to see Jesus. The crowd along the road was so dense he could not push his way to the front; he was too short to see over others' heads. So he climbed a sycamore tree—certainly an undignified thing for a rich and powerful man to do. Jesus saw Zacchaeus, called him down and invited himself to dinner.

Zacchaeus welcomed Jesus by promising to give half his fortune to the poor and to repay four times over anyone he had defrauded. The Law required the Jews to give 10 percent of their income to God. The scribes suggested that a person give 20 percent of his wealth to the poor to show true repentance for dishonesty. This man gave 50 percent. The scribes also required someone who had defrauded another to repay the ill-gotten gains plus 20 percent. This man was willing not only to repay but also to add 400 percent to the repayment.

But Zacchaeus did not promise to give up his job and take to the road with Jesus. His welcoming speech implied that he and his agents would continue to collect the legal toll and no more. He would still be a man of means.

In the chief tax collector we see two character traits of one who wishes to accept Jesus' offer of table fellowship: generosity to the poor and the willingness to make restitution for any unjust or dishonest dealings.

FOR REFLECTION

1) *How do you think the Church should present its need for funds?*

2) *How do you feel when you are asked to give to a second or third collection in Church?*

3) *What percentage of pre-tax income do you think a person should willingly and cheerfully give to the poor? To the Church?*

A Lesson in Humility (Luke 14:1-24)

To look honestly at oneself is very difficult for most people. It is even harder to accept what one sees, the positive and the negative, the weak and the strong, the good and the bad, the present and the absent. Yet Christians invited to take their place at the table of the Lord are expected to come with a true spirit of humility: knowing and accepting themselves, neither comparing themselves to others nor exalting themselves by putting others down. Luke makes this very clear in the table talk which occurs when Jesus has a sabbath dinner at the home of a Pharisee.

Three things occur at this meal which give Jesus the opportunity to make a point. First, a man with dropsy (the result of impurity, according to the Pharisees) looks in at the diners. Jesus cures him and once again makes the point that mercy and concern for the suffering are more important than the observance of the sabbath law.

The second opportunity comes when Jesus noticed how the other guests were selecting their places at table. It was the custom for people to be seated according to their rank and dignity. Each person picked a place in keeping with his own sense of importance. The Pharisees and lawyers felt that they had the right to the highest places, so they jockeyed for positions near the head of the table. Sometimes the host had to rearrange the seating because a person of greater dignity or importance arrived.

Jesus looks at the pushing and the shoving and expresses how he wants his followers to take their places when they come to his banquet. They are to take the lowest places. To be able to do this without resentment or grumbling, they will have to put aside all false and self-righteous claims. They will have to be humble. Then he turns to the host and tells him what kind of people to invite to a banquet: not those who can repay the invitation but the poor, the lame, the outcasts who cannot repay. In other words, Jesus says to be unselfish in hospitality. The ones who will sit close to the Lord at the heavenly banquet will be those who honor all without expecting to be honored, who serve generously without thought of compensation, who give everything and expect nothing.

Opportunity knocks the third time when a lawyer, sensing that Jesus is talking about eating bread in God's Kingdom, applauds him for what he says. Jesus responds by telling a story about a king who threw a banquet. Those who were invited refused to attend at the last minute. Indirectly, Jesus is telling those who would come to his banquet that they cannot allow business interests, care for property or even marriage to interfere with accepting his invitation.

FOR REFLECTION

1) *What are some of the subtle ways good people indulge in pride and self-righteousness?*

2) *Can you recall instances when people stopped doing a good work because they did not receive the recognition they felt they deserved?*

3) *What are modern-day excuses people offer for not coming to the table of the Lord regularly?*

4) *What is the hardest thing for you about coming to the Eucharist?*

Match the Inner and Outer Self (Luke 11:37-54)

It seemed easy 30 or more years ago to know whether or not one was a good Catholic. Mass on Sunday, fish on Friday, one spouse, marriage before a priest, regular confession and prayer, all marked one as a "good" Catholic. These practices satisfied the very natural desire to have some way to know one was on the right track.

Many people think the renewal introduced by Vatican II has muddied the waters. They feel there is too much leeway, too many options. They would prefer to guide their lives by clear-cut norms rather than by intangibles such as love, justice, hope, faith, personal responsibility.

A similar crisis was faced by the Jews a hundred or more years before Christ was born. Because of the inroads of Greek culture, Jewish observance of the Law had become very slack. About 150 B.C. a group of pious Jews began a religious renewal in Israel. They wanted Israel to repent and turn back to God by observing the Law most carefully. Their intention, of course, was to change people's hearts. They thought they could do this by observing the many minute regulations the experts had attached to the Law over the centuries. They put great emphasis on the proper observance of the sabbath, tithing and ritual purity. The followers of this movement at first called themselves "comrades." In time they became known as Pharisees, "those who separate themselves," because they looked down upon and avoided those who did not keep the Law as they did.

By the time Jesus appeared on the scene the movement had lost its inner dynamic and many of the Pharisees were more religious outwardly than inwardly. They had become self-righteous and censorious of other people's way of living. We have to assume that there were many good, sincerely religious people among the Pharisees. Because so many of them were in the forefront of the opposition to Jesus and because in the years after his resurrection they persecuted the Christians, the Gospel writers tend to lump them all together as "bad guys."

One day a Pharisee invited Jesus to take his midday meal with him. Luke does not impute a sinister motive to the invitation. Perhaps the man just wanted to get to know Jesus better and to find out what he was teaching. In this Pharisee's house all the utensils used at the meal were scrupulously clean in accordance with the very detailed regulations on such matters. Everyone except Jesus carefully followed the regulation about washing one's hands before going to the table. This shocked the host. He showed his disapproval. Jesus did not apologize nor explain away his action. Rather he chided those present for thinking that merely following the external rules of purity would make them pure in God's eyes.

This rebuke should serve as a warning to Christians who observe Church laws such as attending Mass or fasting merely because it is a law or because it is a mortal sin to miss Mass. It is also a warning to those who march up the aisle every Sunday to receive Communion without faith or consciousness of the presence of Christ, to those who contribute merely because it is expected of them. Such participation lacks inner authenticity.

Jesus did not say that external practices and observance of the law are useless. Indeed, in Matthew 5:17 he says that he has come to fulfill the law. But he did say that external acts which do not flow from dispositions of justice, love, generous sharing of one's self and almsgiving are valueless as far as God is concerned. In other words, religious practices need to reflect a person's character, the dispositions by which one directs one's life according to the gospel.

The word *Eucharist* means thanksgiving—a clue to the kind of person we are called to be. We are called to be a people who act out of gratitude rather than out of fear. Attendance at the Eucharist is meant to be an external manifestation of a thankful heart. People who are grateful usually express their gratitude in some external way. They are joyful and often are moved to generosity in return. This basic attitude is the basis for the "sacrificial giving" promoted by many parishes. If we are really grateful to God for all he has done for us, we are willing to share what he gives us with his Church and with other charities.

1) Allowing a sum of 10 points for your motives for going to Mass, divide those points among each of the following: gratitude, habit, law, fear, praise of God, asking for favors, other (name). Remember, the points must add up to 10.

2) What one very important reason for being grateful to God impels you to give thanks at Mass?

3) What do you think and how do you feel when you see Catholics who do not live up to the rules and regulations of the Church?

'One Thing Is Necessary' (Luke 10:38-42)

There are few households in which having company for dinner does not cause some tension and upset. There is much to do: set the dining room table, prepare food, set out drinks, clean the house (or at least straighten it up). Usually the hostess is bustling about at the last minute to get things ready. If the rest of the family is parked in front of a TV watching a game, sparks will probably fly.

Jesus walked into just such a situation. We do not know whether Martha had invited him to her home or whether, as a close friend, he just dropped in for supper. In any case Martha had a lot to do.

Setting the table was rather simple in those days: a bowl or plate for each person. They did not use knives, forks or spoons. All usually sat on the floor and ate with their fingers from a common pot.

Getting the meal ready was another question. Martha could not take a few cans off the shelf or frozen food from the freezer. She may have had some cheese, olive oil, honey, wine and grain in the house, but everything else had to be bought at the market from various merchants or farmers. She would have to go from one to another, look over their melons, figs, dates, grapes or raisins, haggle over the price—and then move on to find a fish or a piece of goat or sheep. Then everything had to be cleaned, cut up and prepared. The fire had to be kindled. If she had not already baked that day, there was no fresh bread; she would have to bake it or find a neighbor who would sell her some. There was much to do. No wonder Martha felt burdened when she saw her sister Mary sitting and talking with Jesus.

Martha saw the solution to her problem in other people. If Mary did what she should be doing, there would be no problem. If Jesus told Mary to get into the kitchen, the jobs would get done in time.

Jesus did not buy Martha's solution. Instead he told her to look into herself. She was the source of the problem, and she had the key to the solution. She had worked herself up by fretting about getting a good meal on the table. She could resolve that problem by deciding what was absolutely necessary and what was secondary and of less importance.

Jesus said that one thing only was necessary for hospitality: what Mary was doing. Her hospitality was very personal. She was giving the guest the gift of her presence and of rapt attention to his words. That done, other things would naturally fall into place. They couldn't send out for fried chicken, of course, but there was bound to be some bread and fruit and perhaps a bit of cheese on which they could munch. Better food served up with Mary's attentive love than well-prepared dinners in homes where people welcomed him out of curiosity and listened to his words only in order to trap him.

One more intriguing aspect of this meal story is that it portrays Mary as sitting at the feet of Jesus—a disciple's pose. She is doing something very rare for those days and is not only accepted but also praised for it. It was extremely rare for a woman to be a disciple of a teacher. Yet here and in other cases Jesus accepts women among his followers and his friends.

This story raises some questions about the character of

those who come to table fellowship with the risen Lord. Are they people who realize that the only thing really necessary at Mass is to welcome the Lord and to pay rapt attention to his words? These words are conveyed by the ritual, rephrased in the liturgical prayers, proclaimed in the Scripture readings and expounded in the homily. Or are they busy about many things—the style of the presiding priest and his attention to the rubrics, the music, the behavior of the people on the altar, the decorations in the church, the attention and devotion of the congregation? All these things can distract so much that we cannot calmly, lovingly take our place at the foot of the Lord.

FOR REFLECTION

1) *Most people feel sympathy for Martha but are drawn towards Mary when they come to the Eucharist. Picture a Sunday Mass during which there is much confusion— children running around, people coming late, ministers not knowing what to do and so on. Write to the Lord, finishing these sentences:*

    —*Lord, can't you see what they are doing? I feel* ——.

    —*Tell those people to* ——.

2) *After you have told the Lord how you feel and what you think needs to be changed, listen to his reply. Write down what you hear him say to you.*

3) *What do you believe the role of women in the Church to be today? How do you feel about women on the altar as Eucharistic ministers? As lectors? Servers? Priests? Why do you feel the way you do?*

'Give Them Food Yourselves'
(Luke 9:10-17)

Catholic and Orthodox Christians have always seen the Mass as central to their faith life. In the first century the author of the Letter to the Hebrews wrote, "We must consider how to rouse one another to love and good works. We should not stay away from our assembly, as is the custom of some, but encourage one another..." (Hebrews 10:24-25). The Bishops at Vatican Council II wrote that "the liturgy is the summit toward which the activity of the Church is directed; at the same time it is the fountain from which all her power flows....[It] inspires the faithful to become 'of one heart in love...' " (*Constitution on the Liturgy*, #10).

Of all Luke's meal stories, the feeding of the multitude indicates how important the first Christians felt gathering for the Lord's Supper to be. The only miracle recorded in all four Gospels is this one. (See also Matthew 8:1-10, Mark 6:30-44, John 6:1-15.)

Today a person with a short wave radio can pick up broadcasts from all over the world. If on a certain day stations in England, Russia, China and India were all repeating an incident also being reported by NBC, CBS and ABC, the listener would conclude that it was an important bit of news. But suppose that the simultaneous broadcasts occurred 40 or 50 years *after* the event. A person would conclude that the event was of earth-shattering importance.

Something like this occurs in the Gospels. All four evangelists wrote their accounts of Jesus feeding the multitude from 30 to 60 years after the event. In fact, Mark and Matthew have *two* accounts of such an incident, making six accounts in all. (Mark 8:1-10 and Matthew 15:32-39 are the repeat accounts.)

Jesus may have fed 4,000 people one time and 5,000 another time, but scholars are skeptical. The many similarities in the way the story is told suggest that all six are a record of one event. Scholars tend to agree that Mark had two different accounts of the same event at hand and simply used both of them. Matthew, who drew upon Mark in writing his Gospel, used both accounts.

These accounts differ in details. Scholars explain the differences by indicating the different purpose of the story in each of the Gospels, but all agree that the early Church saw in this event a foreshadowing of the Eucharist. Luke describes Jesus as doing what the Christians did when they celebrated the Lord's Supper: "Then taking the five loaves and the two fish, and looking up to heaven, [Jesus] said the blessing over them, broke them, and gave them to the disciples to set before the crowd" (Luke 9:16).

Look closely at the people in the scene. First watch the crowd. They have come to hear Jesus and to be healed of their ills. Even though they are getting hungry, they are reluctant to break up and go home. We don't know the motives of each person in that multitude, but in general we can say that they manifest an openness to Jesus, a desire to hear something that makes sense out of life, as well as hope for a healing. The sick beg for physical healing, but there must also be those who need healing for the wounds life and sin have inflicted on them. They are a needy bunch—just as we are.

Then observe the apostles. They are concerned for the people but feel impotent. The job Jesus has given them to do—"Give them some food yourselves" (9:13a)—seems far too big for them. They must feel like we do when we hear about the homeless, about the 20,000,000 people living below the poverty level, about the victims of famine and starvation, about war and oppression in all their forms. What Jesus has asked them to do is beyond any capability or resource they can conceive.

Yet they do not shirk the responsibility. Trusting Jesus, they do what he told them to do. They collect five loaves and two fishes, hardly enough to feed themselves and a ridiculous table to set before 5,000. Yet as the loaves and the fishes are passed from person to person, everyone seemed to have enough. In fact, more is left over than they began with.

Here we see people hungry for what Jesus has to offer and men who are humble enough to recognize and admit their limitations. The apostles trust in the power of Jesus in face of an impossible situation. They assume responsibility for meeting the needs of others and are willing to share what little they have.

These attitudes are essential in the character of a Christian. There are many overwhelming problems in life and in the world. Without an attitude of hope, trust and humility, a person can easily fall into cynicism or despair. With such an attitude the Christian does what he or she can do and leaves the rest in the Lord's hands.

FOR REFLECTION

1) *To get a fuller understanding of the meaning of the multiplication of the loaves and fishes, read all four primary accounts (Matthew 8:1-10; Mark 6:30-44; John 6:1-15; Luke 9:10-17). List those elements which are similar in all four and those which are peculiar to each Gospel.*

2) *What do the differences indicate to you about the point each writer emphasized in his version of the story?*

3) *We also gain deeper insight into the story by looking at similar stories in other parts of Scripture. Read one or two of these feeding stories: Exodus 16:4-30; 1 Kings 17:1-14; 1 Kings 19:1-8; 2 Kings 4:1-7; Isaiah 25:6; Isaiah 65:13-21; Psalm 78:19; Psalm 81:16; Acts 2:41-47; Acts 20:7-12; Acts 27:33-38; 1 Corinthians 11:17-22. Indicate the light they shed for you on the story of the feeding of the multitude.*

4) *What insights about the Eucharist do you get from reading all four Gospel accounts as well as one or two other Scripture stories?*

Love and Forgiveness (Luke 7:36-50)

Luke pictures two diverse attitudes of people who sit at the table of the Lord, both of which we may find in ourselves in varying degrees. The negative one—being self-righteous, unconscious of one's own sinfulness and judgmental of others—keeps a person from relating in faith and love to Jesus. The positive attitude—faith, repentance and love—brings a person closer to Jesus and brings the peace Jesus intended to flow from the Eucharist to his friends. Luke presents these attitudes at a dinner party. The person with the positive attitude is a most unlikely person, a prostitute; the owner of the negative attitude is a good solid citizen.

Jesus is invited to dinner by a Pharisee, Simon, who is curious to see whether Jesus really is a prophet. But Simon does not think enough of this wandering rabbi to offer him the ordinary courtesies one offered a guest: He did not have a servant wash Jesus' feet. He gave Jesus no kiss of welcome. He neglected to offer perfume for the hair.

When a streetwalker comes in, Simon and the other "good people" he has invited to dinner immediately jump to conclusions and judge her unfit to be in the company of decent people. The woman Luke pictures is different from their image of her. She is on her knees at the rear of the couch on which Jesus is reclining as he eats. She is washing his feet with her tears, drying them with her hair, kissing them with tender affection and anointing them with an expensive ointment. We do not know what contact she has had with Jesus before this day, but someplace along the line his words and stories, his gentleness and goodness have touched her. She has recognized the sinfulness of her life. In faith she has accepted the forgiveness offered her in love. Now in love she is pouring out signs of her gratitude. Her attitude of recognizing her sin, accepting forgiveness and showing gratitude brings her not only the remission of her sins but also the Lord's peace.

81

These two differing attitudes did not die when Simon and the penitent woman went to their graves. When Luke wrote his Gospel, he no doubt detected both attitudes in the members of his community. The descendants of Simon—judging, stingy, self-righteous—were there as well as grateful, loving, repentant sinners.

Today as we come to the Lord's table we are challenged by this story to look at our own attitudes. It is easy to be self-righteous because we carefully observe the laws of God and the Church. We feel little need for repentance. We feel as though we have *earned* the right to sit at the table of the Lord. It is also easy to feel that we are righteous because our sins can be explained away by heredity, by our upbringing, by psychology, by the fact that everyone is doing it and by the excuse that as long as we feel good about what we are doing it can't be all that bad. This attitude brings no peace, no forgiveness from the Lord.

The attitude which does bring that peace and forgiveness is one which acknowledges sin, sees forgiveness as a gift from God offered in love and shows gratitude by loving acts of kindness for others.

FOR REFLECTION

1) *God's forgiveness of sin depends on our belief that forgiveness is offered and on our acceptance of that offer. What makes it hard for many people to acknowledge the need for God's forgiveness? What makes it hard for many people to forgive themselves?*

2) *There is a bit of the judgmental Simon in most of us. How would spouses show this trait in the way they talk to each other and in the way they talk or feel about their children?*

A Doctor for the Sick (Luke 5:27-39)

One reason some people give for leaving the Church is
that those who do go are "hypocrites who pray to God on
Sunday and prey on their neighbors on Monday." Similarly,
those who are good churchgoers look around the church and
are tempted at times to ask what right the couple living
together or married in violation of Church law have to be
there among the people who keep the law. They are
scandalized when someone known to be engaged in illegal
or dishonest business comes regularly with the family to
Mass. They wonder what good it does for the neighborhood
gossip, the surly troublemaker, the chronic liar, the
perpetual complainer to come to church.

The very first meal story in Luke's Gospel answers all
those people. Jesus, walking along, comes to a customs
house where he sees a tax collector. "Follow me," he says.
Levi gets up and follows him. Then Levi throws a big
banquet for Jesus, inviting all his friends—other tax
collectors. This shocks the scribes and Pharisees, good, law-
abiding Jews who did not associate with sinners such as
dishonest tax collectors.

Perhaps they popped in uninvited to see what Jesus
was up to. (Coming uninvited on a festive occasion was not
a breach in etiquette. From other references in the Bible, it
seems that it was socially acceptable.) Or maybe nosy
neighbors could not avoid seeing and hearing what was
going on because the party flowed out into the courtyard. In
any case, they ask the same question, "Why do you eat and
drink with tax collectors and sinners?" (Luke 5:30b). Jesus'
answer is that the sick, not the healthy, need a doctor.

This story paints a picture of what should be going on
in a healthy Christian community. It cannot be a closed
community limited to the good, the like-minded, the serious
seekers after the Kingdom of God. It must be a community
open to all. It must be a community reaching out to those
beyond the pale or on the outskirts of society. It must be

calling all people and all aspects of society to be healed. A Church which does not address politics, social evils and economic abuses is following in the footsteps of the scribes and Pharisees and saying that certain people or certain aspects of life are not worthy of hearing the Good News.

At the Eucharist Jesus calls to repentance those whose lives are not centered on God, those whose lives are badly missing the mark. The entire Eucharist is a call to repentance, a call to express one's gratitude for God's goodness by changing the way one sees life and the gospel. But this call is most explicit during the penitential rite, when the priest calls *everyone* to ask for God's mercy. All are sinners. No one is worthy to sit at the table of the Lord. All are sick and need a doctor. Perhaps those who think they are not sick are the sickest of all. Jesus came to heal and to bring salvation to all, not to condemn, excommunicate or exclude those who are outcasts, undesirable, alienated from God.

The portrait of a disciple which this scene paints is of a person who is repentant and who tries to reconcile others. It is of one who is not concerned about what others think or about correct social mores when reaching out to those in need of healing. People such as Dorothy Day and Mother Teresa show that the disciple best conveys Jesus' offer of salvation by association rather than by condemnation. The qualities of character this disciple manifests are the same as those Jesus had: compassion, understanding and patience.

FOR REFLECTION

1) *How do you feel when you see people coming to Mass and to Communion who are not observing the laws of the Church or who are openly violating the commandments?*

2) *How do you feel when people of different nationalities or ethnic backgrounds do not act the way you think they should in church?*

3) *How do you feel about babies who cry and children who fidget in church?*

4) *How do you feel about hearing the priest preach on such things as the economy, race relations, nuclear arms?*

Conclusion

The meal stories in Luke taken together paint an ideal picture of the kind of community which should gather to celebrate the Eucharist. The qualities of character this ideal demands are pretty much those of a well-rounded Christian. The reason Luke told these stories was most likely that his community was not living up to this ideal. It does not take a very astute observer to see that such a community has seldom existed.

Nevertheless, the Church has continued to celebrate the banquet of the Lord, the Eucharist, as central to the life of a Christian. Each celebration reminds us what kind of people we are called to be. Within the context of this ritual the Scriptures are proclaimed and explained, but the Eucharist is more than a proclamation of the word. It is a celebration of the presence of the Word. It is a reminder that Jesus is with us, helping us to become what he has called us to be.

FOR REFLECTION

Reflect on this chapter. Then list the qualities of character indicated by Luke's meal stories which you would like to develop more fully in order to find more help and meaning when you sit at the Lord's table.

Chapter Six
The Kingdom

THEOPHILUS LIVED IN A MUCH SIMPLER WORLD than we do. There were no planes, no automobiles, no luxury liners for him. He walked or rode a donkey, and if he crossed the sea it was in an oversized rowboat. People were rich or poor; for all practical purposes there was no middle class. Theophilus did not have to deal with billion-dollar takeovers and their consequences, with Star Wars, with genetic engineering. We will not find many direct answers to the problems we have to face today in the book his friend Luke wrote for him.

But the Second Vatican Council stresses the imperative of "scrutinizing the signs of the times and of interpreting them in the light of the gospel" (*Constitution on the Church in the Modern World*, #4). This is not easily done when we see more than a billion people going to bed hungry every night instead of a mere 5,000 and recall that feeding even that few took a miracle (Luke 16:1-13).

Over the past hundred years the teaching Church has begun to look closely at "the signs of the times" and has begun to indicate ways the Gospel values can be applied to particular social issues. Many people are not convinced that the Church should speak on complex social, economic and political questions. They disagree among themselves about the proper interpretation and application of the gospel to issues which do not seem clear-cut to everyone. Yet in the context of his own culture, Jesus' preaching and actions challenged the social, economic and political practices of his day. He proposed countercultural ideals which the Church today is trying to apply to a world that Theophilus and Luke would never have recognized.

FOR REFLECTION

1) *What 20th-century scientific and technological advances raise new moral questions for us?*

2) *What social, economic, political or technological problems need to be scrutinized in light of the Gospels?*

3) *What are your ideas about the relationship between religion and politics?*

4) *Why do you think so many Catholics have only the vaguest idea of the Church's social teachings?*

'Thy Kingdom Come'

To get a proper perspective on the relation of religion to political, economic and social issues we have to ask, "How does the Kingdom of God come about?" The way believers answer this question determines the extent of their involvement in the world and its problems and their attitudes about the role of the Church in the world.

Christians disagree as to how the Kingdom of God will come about. Some say that it will occur entirely through human effort. Others believe that God brings about the Kingdom entirely alone. A third group believes that human beings are partners with God in bringing about the Kingdom.

The first group, even if they profess something different, will act as though God's Kingdom will come by human action alone. They hold that the world will be gradually and progressively transformed and its evils eliminated when humans fully use their potential for good. They see human beings as potentially self-sufficient and able to obtain salvation through their own efforts. This view is overoptimistic and can lead to excessive pride in human achievement. In the fifth century one of its versions, Pelagianism, was condemned by the Church for putting too much stress on human action and not enough on God's grace and goodness.

A more fundamentalist group believes that only God can bring about the Kingdom and only by once again acting powerfully in the world. They believe that the Kingdom will come when God intervenes and destroys the world as we know it. The elect, the chosen ones, will be lifted up in rapture and God will begin a new, radically different age.

This view sees the world as evil and worthy only of God's destruction. God alone will build the Kingdom; human beings add nothing. Human action at best only expresses longing for the future Kingdom. In this view, one "saves one's soul" or "is saved" through a personal relationship with Jesus without regard for what one does for others. This thinking can lead to believing that work for justice and change is futile, since the world is not worth saving. It can lead to noninvolvement, apathy and even to fatalistic acceptance of things as they are.

The Catholic Church has always tried to hold the middle ground between these two views. It teaches that both God and human beings are necessary for the coming of the Kingdom. Together, as partners, they bring it about. Humans are cocreators with God when they cooperate with divine grace. The bishops at Vatican II put it this way:

> [T]he expectation of a new earth must not weaken but rather stimulate our concern for cultivating this one. For here grows the body of a new human family, a body which even now is able to give some kind of foreshadowing of the new age. Earthly progress must be carefully distinguished from the growth of Christ's

89

Kingdom. Nevertheless, to the extent that the former
can contribute to the better ordering of human society,
it is of vital concern to the Kingdom of God.
(*Constitution on the Church in the Modern World*, #39)

In Luke's view, God's Kingdom is present in some form with
the coming of Christ, but it has to wait till the end of time to
be fully present. In the between-time the Church has to
proclaim by word and deed the presence of the Kingdom
and prepare for its final, complete expression. Jesus
expressed this idea in the parable of the king who goes away
and leaves his servants in charge of his property until he
returns (Luke 19:11-27). The servants can increase or
decrease the king's property depending upon their actions.
It is worth noting that the servants are rewarded on how well
they invest the money entrusted to them by the king.

FOR REFLECTION

1) *Which of these three views of the coming of the kingdom
is closest to your own?*

2) *Read the parable about the absent king (Luke 19:11-27).
What risks did the good servants take? What risks was
the third servant unwilling to take?*

3) *What does this parable suggest about the role of the
bishops and the role of laypeople in the world today?*

4) *What bishops or laypeople do you see taking a risk for
the Kingdom?*

5) *In light of this parable, what would you say to a person
who says that the pope and bishops should stay out of
economical, political and social issues?*

Bearing Witness

Jesus' last admonition to his disciples was that they were to be his witnesses in Jerusalem and throughout the world (Acts 1:8). Earlier he had said, "If anyone wishes to come after me, he must deny himself and take up his cross daily and follow me" (Luke 9:23). Both mandates mean that a disciple must have the same view of life as Jesus, the same value system, the same priorities.

In a world divided into rich and poor, Luke's Jesus has a particular love for the oppressed, the sinner and the outcast. He throws his lot in with them. In his very first recorded sermon he identifies himself as the one sent to proclaim liberty to captives, recovery of sight to the blind and freedom to the oppressed (see Luke 4:18). In the beginning of Luke's Gospel, after agreeing to be his mother, Jesus' first, most nearly perfect disciple proclaims that God:

> ...has thrown down the rulers from their thrones,
> but lifted up the lowly.
> The hungry he has filled with good things;
> the rich he has sent away empty. (1:52-53)

The disciple today must ask whether this attitude of serving love, of concern for the poor and oppressed, applies only on a one-to-one basis or whether it also implies trying to change social, economic and political situations. It is somewhat like the question people concerned about ecology have to ask when seabirds get fouled by an oil spill: "Is it enough to save a few birds by washing and drying them, or do we try to stop the dumping and the oil spills which fouled the birds in the first place?"

1) In our society, whom would you identity as the hungry God will fill with good things (see Luke 1:53)?

2) In our society, whom would you identify as the captives to whom Jesus is sent to proclaim liberty (see Luke 4:18)?

3) In our society, whom would you describe as the blind to whom Jesus promises recovery of sight (see Luke 4:18)?

4) In our society, whom would you identify as the oppressed whom Jesus sets free (see Luke 4:18)?

5) Can you think of any way you might need the freedom about which the Gospel speaks?

Using Money Correctly (Luke 12:20)

Luke's Gospel is not a program of social reform, but it does present basic attitudes necessary to disciples of Jesus. Christians are called to live according to these attitudes and apply them to the social conditions of their times. Basically, this attitude involves self-denial rooted in willingness to live for Christ by loving and reaching out to others in need.

Our generation has to try to live according to this attitude in a world which sets great store on material possessions, in which success is defined in terms of money, in which people are enjoying a material prosperity undreamed of in any other age. We Americans live in a country of great wealth. About four-fifths of us live above the poverty level. In the time of Jesus the reverse was probably true.

Jesus confronted the wealthy of his day, challenging them to be generous and to share their resources with the poor. He saw clearly that wealth may be an obstacle to entering the Kingdom of God. Luke was especially aware of this call to be generous and includes several stories in the Gospel that call for generosity. Three of these stories, the Rich Fool, the Rich Man and Lazarus, and the Good Samaritan, are unique to Luke and address one's use of money. For Luke the love of money was a real concern because he recognized that "You cannot serve God and mammon" (Luke 16:13b).

One can only guess why Luke was so concerned about the correct use of money. Perhaps some of the people whom he and Theophilus knew were so concerned about acquiring money that they needed to be confronted with the challenge to share generously with those in need.

FOR REFLECTION

Read the Beatitudes in Luke 6:20-26 and compare them with those in Matthew 5:3-12.

1) What do these differing accounts suggest to you about the different concrete problems faced by Luke and Matthew?

2) In these readings what does the word poor *suggest to you?*

3) Why do you think Luke's Jesus pronounces those woes on people who are well off?

4) What questions or difficulties does one encounter when trying to put the Beatitudes into practice?

Guarding Against Greed

At the heart of Luke's concern about wealth is one of the seven deadly sins, greed. Greed is an attitude which affects the whole of a person's life. It is the opposite of generosity. Greed is using what one has for one's own advantage. A greedy person is forever discontented, forever craving more. Jesus warned against it: "Take care to guard against all greed, for though one may be rich, one's life does not consist of possessions" (Luke 12:15).

Greed has many forms. It can be excessive desire for money and things. It can be an exaggerated desire to be famous and make a name for one's self or the desire to gain control and call the shots. Greed destroys a person's ability to be open and generous. It brings spiritual death to the greedy person—and sometimes physical death to others when the greedy try to take more and more for themselves. For Luke greed is the primary negative attitude which causes suffering to the victims of the rich and powerful.

Luke makes his point in the parable of the Rich Fool (12:16-21), where Jesus points out how the blinding power of greed kills the spirit of the greedy man. The rich farmer builds his life on false security. He forgets he is mortal and so looks for security in grain and barns. With this false security he lives for himself alone.

The farmer is self-centered and has no concern for others. Six times he uses the word *I* and four times the word *my*. He wants to hold on to his possessions so that he alone can eat, drink and make merry. He does not hold himself accountable to God. In the end the man has neither trust in God nor hope that God will continue his blessings in the future. Unable to share, he has not grown rich in the sight of God. He is a fool.

FOR REFLECTION

1) *In what ways do you see greed as a factor in American life?*

2) *How does this national greed work injustice in other parts of the world?*

3) *In their pastoral letter on the economy, the American*

bishops quoted Pope Paul VI: "Private property does not constitute for anyone an absolute or unconditioned right. No one is justified in keeping for his exclusive use what he does not need, when others lack necessities" (Economic Justice for All, #115). *Explain that statement in your own words. How does this idea apply not only to an individual but to a nation as well?*

Blind Greed

Jesus told another story about a man who did nothing overtly wrong (Luke 16:19-31). The rich man was even a decent sort of fellow, as we can see in his concern for his brothers after his death. His big problem was that he was so blinded by his wealth that he did not even see poor, sick, starving Lazarus at his door.

Jesus' advice to this man can be found in the story of the Dishonest Steward (Luke 16:1-13). Jesus commends the unjust steward who made friends with his master's debtors not because he acted in crisis or because he was dishonest, but because he used money wisely to make friends of those who could help him in time of need. There will come a time when money will have no value, as the rich farmer found out. Then the voices of the poor who have been helped by the correct use of money will have value and power.

FOR REFLECTION

1) *Reread the story of the rich man and Lazarus, substituting the name of a person you consider to be poor in some way for that of Lazarus. What name did you substitute for* Lazarus? *In what ways was your substitute poor (materially, emotionally, physically, spiritually)? What are you doing to alleviate that person's poverty?*

2) *Read the story once again, substituting the words* rich country *for* rich man *and* poor country *for* Lazarus. *What does this parable say about world conditions today?*

Compassion, the Antidote to Greed

Greed prevents one from being open and giving to others. At the same time it prevents one from receiving what God wants to give. The antidote is generosity based on compassion. *Compassion* means to feel with another, to try to walk in the shoes of the other. For this reason Jesus told his followers, "Give to everyone who asks of you, and from the one who takes from you do not demand it back....If you lend money to those from whom you expect repayment, what credit [is] that to you?...[L]end expecting nothing back; then your reward will be great and you will be children of the Most High..." (6:30, 34-35).

Luke also records the story of an official who kept the Law but lacked generosity (Luke 18:18-23). When he asked how to obtain eternal life, Jesus told him to keep the commandments. This the official said he had done. Then Jesus told him that there was still one more thing to do: "[S]ell all that you have and distribute it to the poor, and you will have a treasure in heaven." But the official went away sad, for he was very rich.

The response of the official was in direct contrast to that of Barnabas, who sold his farm and gave the money to the apostles to be used for the poor (see Acts 4:36-37). Barnabas went on to become a great missionary, St. Paul's friend and traveling companion.

Perhaps the most powerful message about the generous use of one's resources is found in another parable which is also unique to Luke, the story of the Good Samaritan (Luke 10:29-37).

A priest, a Levite and a Samaritan all travel the road

96

between Jerusalem and Jericho. All three see the same injured individual, yet only one is moved to pity. He alone shows compassion and proves to be a true and good neighbor. Perhaps the other two felt that they did not have the time or the energy to get involved. Perhaps they were so wrapped up in their business that they did not notice him. In any case, for reasons good or bad, they walked by, and only one stopped to help.

Jesus' challenge to us is, "Go and do likewise."

The economics pastoral of the American bishops presents the challenge to involvement as a quest. We must seek out those in need, they say:

> The quest for economic and social justice will always combine hope and realism, and must be renewed by every generation. It involves diagnosing those situations that continue to alienate the world from God's creative love as well as presenting hopeful alternatives that arise from living a renewed creation. This quest arises from faith and is sustained by hope as it seeks to speak to a broken world of God's justice and love. (*Economic Justice for All*, #55)

FOR REFLECTION

1) *Who in the Church is primarily responsible for diagnosing alienating situations and presenting hopeful alternatives?*

2) *What would be the most helpful form of collaboration among laypeople, the bishops and the clergy in carrying out the pastoral's "quest"?*

3) *The bishops' economics pastoral states that the challenge of Jesus "demands a compassionate vision that enables the church to see things from the side of the poor and powerless, and to assess life-style, policies and social institutions in terms of their impact on the poor"* (Economic Justice for All, #52). *The bishops call this*

a "preferential option for the poor."
How do you feel when your bishop and all the other bishops together give top priority to the poor and the neglected in our society?
How does the bishops' statement challenge the Church's life-style? Your parish's life-style?
How does their statement challenge your life-style?
What do you think you might do differently as a result of reflecting on Luke's emphasis on justice and concern for the poor?

4) What insights on social justice have you gained from this chapter?

Postscript

OUR EXPLORATION OF LUKE is finished. We have offered but one way to read his Gospel, concentrating on his stories. We have not examined these stories in a scholarly way but in a pastoral way, a way that seeks to embody them in the hearer's everyday life.

We hope that this book will encourage you to delve more deeply into the Gospel of Luke as well as into the other three Gospels. The Good News is of no value buried in a book. It must be lived as fully as possible in order to be Good News to us personally.

FOR REFLECTION

Go back to the questions on pages 5-6. See if you answer them now in the same way you did when you began to read this book.

Bibliography

Barclay, William. *The Gospel of Luke*. The Daily Study Bible Series, Vol. 4. Philadelphia: Westminster Press, 1975.

Bright, Laurence, ed. *Luke: Gospel, Acts, 1 Peter*. Scripture Discussion Commentary, Vol. 8. Chicago: ACTA Publications, 1971.

Kodell, Jerome, O.S.B. *The Gospel According to Luke*. Collegeville Bible Commentary: New Testament Series, Robert J. Karris, O.F.M., ed., Vol. 5. Collegeville, Minn.: The Liturgical Press, 1983.

Little Rock Scripture Study Program. Collegeville, Minn.: The Liturgical Press.

Mackenzie, J.L., ed. *The New Testament for Spiritual Reading*, Vol. 5, *Gospel According to Luke, Part 1*. New York: Crossroad, 1981.

———.Vol. 6, *Gospel According to Luke, Part 2*. New York: Crossroad, 1981.

Obach, Robert E. with Albert Kirk. *A Commentary of the Gospel of Luke*. Mahwah, N.J.: Paulist Press, 1986.